"In *Passionate Pursuit*, Jason Chatraw pushes past popular clichés to inspire us with a biblical, authentic faith. The section on 'Powerful Prayer' in particular challenged me to re-evaluate my own honesty and openness with God. The questions are thoughtful and provoking, providing a life-transforming study."

— *Gary L. Thomas, author of*
Seeking the Face of God *and* Sacred Pathways

PASSIONATE

PURSUIT

Discovering the Heart of Christ

JASON CHATRAW

Atlanta Vineyard
Publishing

Norcross, Georgia 30071
www.avpublishing.com

Published by Atlanta Vineyard Church
Atlanta Vineyard Publishing
6920 Jimmy Carter Blvd.
Suite 200
Norcross, GA 30071

To order, visit the website at: www.avpublishing.com

Cover design by Swing from the Rafters. Visit their website at: www.swingfromtherafters.com

Printed in the United States of America

<u>Anthony</u>

Ayley

Drug bust

<u>James</u>

Duchess Palmer

<u>Randy</u>

"Burn out"

F G H

Ayley – girlfriend – breat up

Laura – Nashville? → MTS – MBA

Mom – graduation 2:30

Angie   Reeves – young 19 son – funeral

<u>Richard</u>

Sarah McClelland – traveling nurse
                    Miami – Lupus?

Gayle + Richard
                    sore on foot
Pat Felise

Bldg. project – blessing

DeLancey

<u>Ed</u>

Ray Matthews

Mother – – almost blocked out

Lance

Nephew – grad – ~~Gr~~ Jarod Hale

Contents

Dedication

To my beautiful wife, Janel, for the way she encourages me to pursue my relationship with God, and to my parents, Darrell and Margaret, for instilling in me a passion to pursue God at an early age

Author's Foreword

Before I ever thought of writing anything for public viewing related to having a relationship with God, a friend of mine named David Herndon encouraged me to let other people read what I was writing. Not long after that, I began compiling devotionals that I wrote following my daily time with the Lord. In 1999, on a whim, I began sending a devotional e-mail to a friend of mine who began forwarding them on to other believers. Before long, it became a daily staple for a large number of people.

I never imagined that God would use my writing to encourage people in their relationship with Him, but it's amazing what God will do when we yield to His plans and purposes.

My prayer for you as you read this book is that God will speak to you and that you will be challenged to follow Him with more zeal and passion than you ever have in your life. A leisurely pursuit of God will prevent us from tapping into the fullness of life that He has for us. However, when we passionately pursue Him, we find unspeakable joy as we enter into the adventure of a lifetime.

As this book encourages and challenges you in your relationship with God, embrace the challenge. God's adventure for you awaits.

Identity in Christ

If I find in myself a desire which no experience in this world can satisfy, the most probable explanation is that I was made for another world.
– C.S. Lewis

Day One: Who We Are

In an attempt to find ourselves, we get lost. "Who am I?" we each ask, wondering if we're the only one with that question. And regardless of what we're told, it's difficult for us to believe what we see in front of us: we are children of God — loved unconditionally, redeemed at the highest of prices.

PursuingGod'sWord
2 Corinthians 5:16-17

The morning started out as every other morning for Saul: he was on a mission to stop the spreading of this allegiance to Jesus Christ. There is no way he suspected that before this encounter with God was finished that he would have a totally different outlook on his life.

We don't have to look any further for who we are — we are new creatures.

But before he knew it, Saul was on his face, crying out to the Lord. "Who are You, Lord?" Saul asked as he fell to the ground. (Acts 9:5) And it was the beginning of the end for Saul — the end of his tiring persecution act, the end of his skewed mission, the end of his emptiness. This was the end of Saul.

Not only did the Lord answer Saul's question, he concluded this confrontation by showing Saul who he was now: his name was now Paul and he was a new creation in Christ.

It didn't take long for Paul to realize both his new name and his new calling in life. Neither did it take long for Paul to realize who he truly was: a child of God. In fact, he recognized this so fast that he wasted no time in telling others about the saving power of the Gospel. "Immediately he preached the Christ in the synagogues, that He is the Son of God. Then all who heard were amazed" (Acts 9:20-21).

The moment we come to Christ, we assume a new identity. No longer are we wretched creatures, but we are men and women of God. We are His children.

This amazing encounter with God probably heavily influenced Paul when he wrote this passage in 2 Corinthians 5:16-17: "Therefore, from now on, we regard no one according to the flesh. Even though we have known Christ according to the flesh, yet now we know Him thus no longer. Therefore, if anyone is in Christ, he is a new creation; old things have passed away; behold, all things have become new." We don't have to look any further for who we are. God spells it out for us: we are new creatures. We are His.

As we begin to take this truth to heart, we realize that it doesn't matter what we do or where we work. It doesn't matter where we've been or where we're headed. Our identity should no longer be linked solely to our jobs, or anything else for that matter — relationships, family, money, power, fame.

We are children of God. He loves us without condition. There's nothing we can do to please Him more or make Him love us more — nothing. We are His, and His alone.

Christ's Heart in You

1. If someone asked you to describe yourself, what would you say?

2. From what types of things do you derive your identity?

Pray: "Lord, help me to see myself the way You created me and realize that my identity is in You. Amen."

<><

Day Two: God's Love

If ever there was a time to wallow in self-disappointment for Peter, this was the time. Over the course of a few days, he watched his

Pursuing God's Word
John 21:1-14

beloved friend Jesus wrestle with His fate in the Garden of Gethsemane, denied Christ three times, and doubted that He would rise from the grave. "I'm such a failure," Peter surely thought to himself. "I wasn't even a good friend to Jesus."

But God views our failures differently. While we may use them as a chance to bash our already battered self-esteem, God sees them as a chance to extend His grace into our lives. To the truly repentant, there is no greater example of God's loving nature than to be restored after failing miserably.

Despite his failures, Peter understood who he was — and he understood who Jesus was. Peter knew that the Lord was not going to turn His back on him and walk away, even though that action would've been completely justified. But Peter understood a concept we so desperately need to grasp in our relationship with Jesus Christ: no matter what we do, God's love for us is constant.

When Peter saw Jesus following His resurrection, his failures were a distant memory — as he knew they would be to Jesus as well. "Therefore that disciple whom Jesus loved said to Peter, 'It is the Lord!' Now when Simon Peter heard that it was the Lord, he put on his outer garment (for he had removed it), and plunged into the sea" (John 21:7).

Peter swam to Jesus because he was so excited to see Him again. Forget the three denials, forget falling asleep in the garden — Jesus was back, and Peter loved Him and knew he was loved by Him. Oswald Chambers writes, "Beware of succumbing to failure as inevitable; make it the stepping-stone to success."

To the truly repentant, there is no greater example of God's loving nature than to be restored after failing miserably.

Instead of viewing himself as a failure for not sticking close by Jesus' side during the most difficult time in His life, Peter learned a few valuable lessons. He saw that following Jesus wasn't going to be easy, but it was what He truly desired to do. Peter also realized that no matter how many times he fell flat on his face, Jesus loved him dearly.

Our identity is not based on how many times we fail or succeed — it is based simply on Christ. He loves us no matter what we do, but our goal should be to serve and honor Him with all our hearts and souls and minds as we discover what it means to truly love God with all our being.

Never should our failures confirm deep suspicions we have about ourselves. Instead, our failures should be viewed as opportunities to see God's loving hand of grace extended into our lives, for we are His children.

Christ's Heart in You

1. When you sin, how do you feel about yourself? How do you think God feels about you?

2. How can you take your moments of weakness and learn from them? What have you already learned from past mistakes?

Pray: "Lord, help me to see Your unfailing love for me even when I fall in following You."

<><

Day Three: Our Purpose

Deep in his heart, the writer wanted to do nothing more than please God. He desired to serve the Lord with all that was in him, but he wanted to know the best way to do so. He knew that he was created to write, to encourage others in their faith through the Gospels, but there had to be more. So, he went to Jesus for the answer to his tormenting question.

> **PursuingGod'sWord**
> Mark 12:28-34

We too must realize that our purpose is to love God.

"Then one of the scribes came, and having heard them reasoning together, perceiving that He had answered them well, asked Him, 'Which is the first commandment of all?' Jesus answered him, 'The first of all the commandments is: Hear, O Israel, the Lord our God, the Lord is one. And you shall love the Lord your God with all your heart, with all your soul, with all your mind, and with all your strength. This is the first commandment'" (Mark 12:28-30).

And suddenly, the lights came on for this inquisitive scribe. He realized that, despite what his function was on earth, his ultimate purpose and calling in life was to love God. He finally found it! His life would no longer be steeped in monotonous academia, but now he would demonstrate his deep love for God in every aspect of his life. His life would be an example of devoted love for the Lord!

So often in life we relate who we are with what we do. We base our identity off some warped sense of function and totally miss what God really wants from us. He simply wants us to love Him back. It's what makes His heart sing. It's what makes His heart leap over us. It's what makes Him smile as He watches us from heaven.

It's just that easy, but we tend to complicate the matter. We want this grand formula of how we should serve Him and desire Him to hand us a course that contains our lives plotted out before us. We quickly forget that God simply wants our love. He is constantly calling us to come home, to follow Him, to love Him, yet we get wrapped up in the insignificant details of life and lose our way.

Just like this scribe realized his purpose in life, we too must realize that our purpose is to love God. He has already humbled Himself and sacrificed His only Son just so we could have fellowship with Him. And He's not asking or demanding us to do anything — He is inviting us to join in the greatest journey that we can ever know.

This journey all starts when we realize we are His children and that all He wants from us is our love. He is waiting for us to accept His invitation and find this high, yet simple, purpose for us: love Him back.

Christ's Heart in You

1. What sense of purpose do you have in your life? How does your relationship with God fit into that purpose?

2. How can you demonstrate your love for God in your life?

Pray: "Lord, help me to realize that loving You is my purpose, to honor You is to live for You."

<><

Day Four: Our Dependency

As Peter began to realize who he was in Christ, he also began to realize that his way of living was quite faithless and independent from God. As he began to understand that there was more to this life than what he had been experiencing, the floodgates of heaven opened up in Peter's life.

On his way to the temple at gate Beautiful, Peter had seen this

PursuingGod'sWord
Acts 3:1-10

lame beggar's tired act many times before this day. But this wasn't just any old day, and Peter had grown weary of acting as if he didn't believe his friend Jesus' teachings.

We can only lean on a God we trust.

"Then Peter said, 'Silver and gold I do not have, but what I do have I give you: In the name of Jesus Christ of Nazareth, rise up and walk.' And he took him by the right hand and lifted him up, and immediately his feet and ankle bones received strength. So he, leaping up, stood and walked and entered the temple with them — walking, leaping, and praising God; and they were filled with wonder and amazement at what had happened to him" (Acts 3:6-8, 10).

Peter knew that this power surging within his veins was not his own — he knew where it came from. And he decided it was time to tap into that power and begin depending on it to change his life and the lives of others.

Everything began to become clear for Peter. He recognized that if he was willing to depend on God, the Lord would show up and demonstrate His power. After all, there was no need to argue with this exercise of faith — it was the same way Jesus lived His life. Paul writes, "Imitate me, just as I also imitate Christ" (1 Corinthians 11:1).

So, how did Christ live? He lived dependent upon God for His next breath. He looked to His heavenly Father for assistance in every trying circumstance and situation in life. He understood that God the Father desired the best for His life. But do we?

How willing are we to begin to live in a state of dependency upon God? Do we understand who we are in Christ — that we are God's children — so that we can grasp the concept that He does want the best for us? Regardless of what kind of family we come from, does it register within our minds that our heavenly Father truly wants to give us everything He has in mind for our lives?

We can only lean on a God we trust. If we don't trust that this is truly what God wants for our lives — His best in every circumstance — then how can we depend upon Him completely? We can't. We must first realize that He desires to give us more than we could ever possibly conceive. Then and only then can we start to live with our faith resting squarely upon His shoulders, knowing that He will indeed remain true to His Word.

Christ's Heart in You

1. In what ways do you live in dependency upon God? What other areas can you depend upon Him more?

2. How would you characterize your trust in God? Explain why you trust Him to the level you do.

Pray: "Lord, help me to depend upon You more in areas of my life that I struggle to surrender to You."

<><

Day Five: No Condemnation

In our relationship with Christ, the only condemnation we feel is from ourselves. The Holy Spirit will convict us of our sin, but He never condemns us for what we have done. Instead, God touches our hearts with His grace and forgiveness.

> **PursuingGod'sWord**
> John 8:1-11

It was a whirlwind of events for this young woman who had been caught red-handed in the lustful arms of a married man. While the two were both at fault, she was the target of condemnation by the scribes and Pharisees on this chosen afternoon.

Chasing this ashamed woman through the streets, the Pharisees decided they would test Jesus. "Surely there is no way this promoter of grace can maintain His rhetoric without spitting on the laws of God," they thought to themselves. They thought they had Jesus cornered. "Teacher, this woman was caught in adultery, in the very act. Now Moses, in the law, commanded us that such should be stoned. But what do You say?" (John 8:4-5).

The proverbial line had been drawn in the sand, or so the Pharisees thought. There is no reconciling grace and the law: Jesus would either condemn her, departing from His teachings of grace; or He would pardon her, shirking the laws of Moses.

But Jesus, as He did so many times, brought God's law and His redemptive plan together for a beautiful merger that sang harmoniously with the true heart of His heavenly Father: "He who is without sin among you, let him throw a stone at her first" (John 8:7).

There it was, laid before the Pharisees for them to see. While God's law was set up for a reason, His grace ran much deeper. In an instant, we see the heart of God for all of mankind, particularly His children.

God's heart breaks when we sin but rejoices when we turn back to Him to be restored.

God desires to draw us to Himself, not to turn us away. He doesn't want to slam the gavel and pronounce us condemned, delivering a sentence that condemns us. Rather, God's heart breaks when we sin but rejoices when we turn back to Him to be restored. He is forever calling us, never giving up on His children.

Condemnation merely heaps shame upon one's head, but love births the life that was purposed by God. He doesn't want to see us wallow in the death of sin, but live victoriously through Christ. As we grasp our identity in Christ, we must also grasp the heart of the heavenly Father. For it is there that we see the way in which He desires to lavish His love upon His children. "There is therefore now no condemnation to those who are in Christ Jesus, who do not walk according to the flesh, but according to the Spirit" (Romans 8:1).

Christ's Heart in You

1. How do you handle conviction when you feel the Holy Spirit revealing an area in your life that needs some extra attention?

2. How do you respond when you see God's mercy win out over judgment in your own life? In other's lives?

Pray: "Lord, help me to live in the fullness of Your grace, extending a heart of grace to those who sin against me."

<><

Your Pursuit

Powerful Prayer

We must alter our lives in order to alter our hearts,
for it is impossible to live one way and pray another.
— William Law

Day One: Pure Motives

In a world riddled with mistrust and decep-
tion, it's difficult to believe people who come
to us with propositions that appear too good
to be true. We wonder if they really want to do something for us out of the
"goodness of their heart" because we wonder just how much goodness
really exists. We ask ourselves if they are here because they want to bless
us or because they want to get something from us.

> **PursuingGod'sWord**
> 1 Samuel 1:19-28

     Even though we acknowledge that God knows our hearts, we
sometimes approach Him as if He doesn't know, as if we're going to trick
Him into giving us what we want by acting sincere and genuine. But God
knows why we are before Him. Maybe it's because we aren't getting our
way. Maybe it's because we dislike the discomfort pressing on our lives.
Maybe it's because we think He needs to align His plans with ours.

     When we go before the Lord in prayer, making our requests
known to Him, we must first ask ourselves why we are asking this of Him.
And if it's ultimately for His glory that we ask, we can rest assured that our
hearts are pure.

     Hannah loved God with all her heart, yet she was broken over the
fact that she could have no children. While her motherly instincts yearned
to have a child, she so desperately wanted to give something of herself to
the Lord. And she was willing to give God the most precious thing she
could think of if she ever received him: her son.

In her prayers to the Lord, Hannah said that she would give her son to Him for His service alone. And God granted her request, giving her Samuel. Hannah, too, followed through with her promise and dedicated Samuel to the Lord's service.

How many times do we ask for things so that we can give them back to God?

Hannah said, "For this child I prayed, and the Lord has granted me my petition which I asked of Him. Therefore I also have lent him to the Lord; as long as he lives he shall be lent to the Lord" (1 Samuel 1:27-28). While Hannah faithfully gave of herself to God, she wanted to give something to Him that meant the world to her. But she couldn't. She wanted to dedicate her son to the Lord, but she had no son to give.

So pure was Hannah's prayer that she didn't even ask for this gift for herself, but she asked for a son for the Lord. How many times are our prayers reflective of this selfless, God-centered mentality? How many times do we ask for things so that we can give them back to God?

Hannah rejoiced and celebrated over this wonderful gift the Lord had given her. And she gave it right back to Him without hesitation. It was in her heart to do so. When we come before God with a pure heart — one devoid of all selfish motivation — we will be able to see His heart for us and ask, not for our own sakes, but for His glory.

Christ's Heart in You

1. When you pray, what motivates your requests to God?

2. What are some things you can request of God so you can give them back to Him?

Pray: "Lord, I want to honor You with my life. Purify my heart and mind so that my desires are Your desires."

<><

Day Two: Honest Confession

Instead of conversation with the Lord, sometimes our prayers transform into a laundry list of items we want corrected. There is no deep honesty in our prayers; rather, it's a wish list that we present before God. We don't listen for His response. We don't wait for His guidance. We don't do anything but convey our desires and leave.

PursuingGod'sWord
Psalm 55:1-5

In light of God's omniscience, we often think it is foolish to tell Him how we feel. After all, shouldn't the God of the universe, the God who knows how many hairs are on our heads, know how we feel at any given time?

Prayer, the kind that communes with God and changes our world in the process, is honest. It is an expression of our hearts, not a list from our heads. Surely God knows every thought we have during the day, but why not share those with Him? Why treat Him as if He is some far-off deity that isn't interested in every aspect of our lives?

Known as a man after God's own heart, King David understood how honest confession before the Lord took a time of prayer from being static to extremely dynamic. As David shared his thoughts, his fears, his hopes, and his dreams, he communed with God on the most intimate level. His prayers didn't drone away into the night — they took flight and resulted in action by his heavenly Father.

Prayer is an expression of our hearts, not a list from our heads.

Consider this psalm David wrote: "Give ear to my prayer, O God, and do not hide Yourself from my supplication. . . . My heart is severely pained within me. Fearfulness and trembling have come upon me, and horror has overwhelmed me" (Psalm 55:1,4-5).

How willing are we to be honest and vulnerable before God like that? This wasn't a gripe session for David — this was an opportunity for him to open up before the Lord and show Him what was in his heart. David was getting very real before the Lord because he knew that honesty was the only way to God's heart.

Today, we have the Holy Spirit — the Spirit of Truth — leading and guiding our lives. And as honesty begins to encompass our entire lives, we must not limit it to certain portions of our Christian walk. Honesty should become so ingrained into our hearts that it flows from our lips as we talk with the Lord. He is seeking authentic people who aren't afraid to tell Him when they are afraid or when something has heavily burned their hearts.

David concludes his psalm by saying, "Cast your burden on the Lord, and He shall sustain you; He shall never permit the righteous to be moved" (Psalm 55:22). As we get honest before the Lord, we will watch our fears and burdens vanish as He replaces those parts of our hearts with His assurance.

Christ's Heart in You

1. How honest do you feel you are when you pray?

2. In what areas can you be more open and honest with God when you are before Him in prayer?

Pray: "Lord, I know You know my heart, but I want to present all of me as I am before You. Use me as You see fit."

<><

Day Three: Cries for Help

When trials disrupt our lives and back us into the tightest of corners, we sometimes want to shake an angry fist at

> PursuingGod'sWord
> Exodus 4:1-31

God. And why not? We assume that if God is truly sovereign, then He allowed this dreadful situation to take place — and we want to know why.

Our cry for help isn't a cry at all — it's an accusation against God. We cast blame on Him for not steering and directing us to an easier, safer place. In fact, we don't even cry out for help; we simply cry out "why?" But is this what prayer should look like in our most dire moments in life?

Moses found himself in the middle of one of the greatest moments in Old Testament history. By the almighty power of God, Moses had led God's people out of captivity in Egypt and into the wilderness. From there, the people would enter the promised land, but for now, there was a lot of ground to put between them and a fast-closing Egyptian army.

Pharaoh quickly changed his mind and the Egyptian army bore down on the Israelites in the wilderness. So, there stood Moses, the crucial link between God and the people — the man who could lead these people to their destiny or into failure. Moses, however, was not destined to fail.

His cry to God was one of confidence and assurance, not panicked fear like the people.

"Then they said to Moses, 'Because there were no graves in Egypt, have you taken us away to die in the wilderness? Why have you so dealt with us, to bring us out of Egypt?'" (Exodus 14:11).

But Moses' response demonstrated where his faith rested: "Do not be afraid. Stand still, and see the salvation of the Lord, which He will accomplish for you today. For the Egyptians whom you see today, you shall see again no more forever" (v. 13).

The next time the walls begin to close around us, we must remember where to place our trust and faith.

Moses' cry for help was one that resembled trust and strength found only in the Lord. God does not lead us out of a dire situation into something even more desperate and hopeless. His heart for us is of love and always for the best. But our short memories forget the last demonstration of His faithfulness in our lives, and we return to a cry of blame, not a cry for help.

In the midst of his calm, assuring words to the Israelites, Moses was really saying, "God, I know You can do this and I know You didn't lead us here to die. Please do something immediately that will demonstrate Your power to both the people and the Egyptians."

That is a cry for help; the type of cry that acknowledges God's saving power and asks for Him to both save us and point others to the truth. The next time the walls begin to close around us, we must remember where to place our trust and faith, crying out for God, not in a way that blames Him for our situation, but looks to Him for our salvation.

Christ's Heart in You

1. What are your prayers like when you are in the midst of a crisis?

2. The next time you need to cry out for help, how can you do so in a way that shows where your trust is?

Pray: "Lord, I know You deliver me from all evil in my life. Continue to hold me close to You."

<><

Day Four: Openness with God

Pursuing**God's**Word
Matthew 26:36-46

Bottling up things inside us has the tendency to make us highly irritable as well as develop bitterness and anger toward the person or situation about which we keep mum. Bitter Christians might be one of the biggest turnoffs to the faith as their venom spews forth years later. By withholding their feelings from God and others, the anger builds, making its entrance into the world that much more powerful.

Although we know Jesus experienced the same feelings and emotions as we do, it is hard for us to conceive of how He felt at times. Yet, like all of us, when situations developed into something nearly unbearable, He felt it and didn't necessarily want to experience it.

Jesus knew that His ultimate purpose in the world was to lead mankind to redemption, to cleanse a world mired in their sin. But He also knew that with that redemption came a price that only He could pay — that of death on the Cross.

Jesus' openness with His Father demonstrates how openness in prayer leads to God's perfect will.

In the Garden of Gethsemane hours before His arrest, Jesus prayed with His disciples. Distanced from Peter, James, and John, Jesus fell on His face before God. The anguish in His voice had to pierce His words: "O My Father, if it is possible, let this cup pass from Me; nevertheless, not as I will, but as You will" (Matthew 26:39).

Three times Jesus cried out to God. This wasn't a criminal pleading for a stay of His execution — this was the Son of God pleading for God to intervene if at all possible. Ultimately, Jesus wanted to do His Father's will, but He was also asking if there was any other way to accomplish God's will without Him dying this excruciating death and being separated from His Father.

Jesus' openness with His Father demonstrates how openness in prayer leads to God's perfect will, allowing us to accept His plan with full confidence and assurance. Surely God's heart ached as He heard His Son crying out, but God's heart also ached for all of mankind and He knew that this was the only way. He knew that Jesus would be taken care of and that it would be the best for Him and everyone else in the end.

In our prayers, we must not be afraid to be open with God. Yes, He knows how we are feeling and knows our every thought, but to fear telling Him what's on our hearts and minds is the beginning of bitterness. Instead of willingly accepting His plans for us, we sneer in disgust and wonder why He would do such a terrible thing to us.

Jesus made no demands of His Father through this difficult situation; rather, He expressed His heart and affirmed His commitment to God by saying, "Your will be done." In opening up before the Lord, we should feel free to express our fears and concerns, yet knowing that in the end what He allows us to endure will be the best.

Christ's Heart in You

1. Whenever you are faced with difficulty in life, how open are you in your prayers to God?

2. In what ways can you be more open about your feelings with God in prayer?

Pray: "Lord, give me the courage to express my heart fully to You in every situation in my life."

Day Five: The Model of Jesus

T oo often in life, original ideas and thoughts are distorted by vague replications. The replication may be good, but a replication of another replication leads to only further deterioration. That is true of many things in our lives, including how we view other believers. While it is good to see someone who is patterning his or her life after Christ, we should be careful to imitate Christ, not the person we see.

PursuingGod'sWord
Luke 11:1-13

The same is true for our prayer lives. As we began to turn our lives over to God, we began to pray. And many times, we learned to pray from those other trusted believers around us. Not always was their example a true reflection of the way Christ taught His disciples to pray.

"One of His disciples said to [Jesus], 'Lord, teach us to pray, as John also taught his disciples.' So He said to them, 'When you pray, say . . .'" (Luke 11:1-2).

Instead of droning away some prayer that bears no meaning to us, we must look carefully at what Jesus was saying and be diligent about applying it to our prayer life. Undoubtedly, every time Jesus went before His Father in prayer, He did not churn out these words. Instead, He used this opportunity to teach His disciples the outline for powerful prayer.

As we enter into conversation with God, we should recognize the blessings He has given us.

"Our Father in heaven, hallowed be Your name" begins Jesus' model prayer, teaching us to acknowledge God as our Father and also to praise Him. Psalm 100:4 says we should "enter His courts with praise." As we enter into conversation with God, we should recognize the blessings He has given us. We should always go before Him with a grateful heart.

"Your kingdom come, Your will be done on earth as it is in heaven" is the portion of our prayer where we confess that God's values are our own. Romans 14:17 says that the kingdom of God is "righteousness and peace and joy in the Holy Spirit." We should ask God to make those three elements of His character present in our lives, as we also ask Him to do His will within us and through us in every situation.

"Give us day by day our daily bread, and forgive us our sins, as we also forgive everyone who is indebted to us" leads us to asking God for provision in certain areas of our lives as well as showing us just how important forgiveness is — both to Him and to those around us.

"And do not lead us into temptation, but deliver us from the evil one" is our cry for protection from the enemy as he tries to thwart God's plans for our lives. We should be diligent in asking the Lord to protect us and deliver us.

As this prayer shows, God is interested in all aspects of our lives — from the deeply spiritual to our every human need. Let us become a people devoted to prayer that changes things, both in our lives and in the world around us.

Christ's Heart in You

1. How would you describe your prayer life? Mundane? Dynamic? Explain why.

2. What elements of the Lord's prayer can you better incorporate into your daily prayer life?

Pray: "Lord, instill in me a passion for prayer and don't let it become something I feel obligated to do. Give me a desire to seek You in prayer."

Your Pursuit

Called to Serve

---

*Start by doing what's necessary; then do what's possible;
and suddenly you are doing the impossible.*
— St. Francis of Assisi

Day One: The Mission

PursuingGod'sWord
Judges 6:11-16

Stricken with fear of the oppressive Midianites, Gideon stole away quietly to a winepress — but his intention wasn't to make wine. In the winepress, Gideon threshed wheat. He knew that if the Midianites saw what he was doing, he quite possibly could die after they took his wheat.

Crouched in this vat threshing wheat, Gideon's appearance didn't exactly strike anyone as that of being a great "leader." However, this is how the angel of the Lord found him. Obviously, Gideon struggled with fear, but that was merely the beginning. There was insecurity to combat, along with feelings of doubt and inadequacy.

But before the angel even unveiled God's plan for Gideon, he exhorted Gideon with these words: "The Lord is with you, you mighty man of valor!" (Judges 6:12). Crouched in a vat threshing wheat? This was a mighty man of valor?

God sees beyond all our inadequacies, all our weaknesses. In fact, He views them as windows of opportunity to demonstrate His amazing grace and power in our lives. There's no fault so deep in our character that His strength can't overcome it.

While Gideon was skeptical about why an angel would appear to him in the first place, the angel delivered the message: "Go in this might of yours, and you shall save Israel from the hand of the Midianites. Have I not sent you?" (Judges 6:14).

Gideon? Save Israel from the Midianites? Did this angel truly see

29

the picture in front of him? Gideon was huddled in a winepress vat thresh-ing wheat out of fear of the Midianites, not because he was a mighty man of valor by the world's standards. And this was the man who was going to save Israel?

God doesn't call us to do things we can do on our own apart from Him.

Gideon even balked at the notion that he could do such a thing. He knew that he was incapable of doing this on his own, which is why the Lord quickly comfort-ed Gideon with these words: "Surely I will be with you" (Judges 6:16).

God doesn't call us to do things we can do on our own apart from Him. God used Gideon because he was willing — even if it took a little prodding to con-vince him that God would be with him.

When we think we can accomplish much on our own without God, we must realize that the potential to see more happen occurs when we return to Him the life He has called us to live and give Him the things He has asked us to give.

Our weaknesses are obstacles that God will overcome as we open our lives to Him. All throughout Scripture, we see God using weak men to move mountains. David was a shepherd boy with a penchant for killing animals with a slingshot, but God infused supernatural strength in him to kill a giant. Peter was an established fisherman, but God used him to har-vest souls for His Kingdom.

And God will use us too. Amidst all our weaknesses and inadequa-cies, God will transform our willing hearts into strong hands of valor.

Christ's Heart in You

1. What fears do you have in your life when it comes to serving God with all your heart?

2. What things do you feel God is nudging you to do that seem overwhelm-ing? Why do they seem that way?

Pray: "Lord, fill my heart with courage to pursue You and Your direction for my life, no matter what it is."

<><

Day Two: Practical Steps

The directive was clear: save Israel from the Midianites. All Gideon wanted to know then was how he was supposed to accomplish this. So, as he listened to the Lord's voice for instruction, the first step didn't seem like much of a step at all.

"The Lord said to [Gideon], 'Take your father's young bull, the second bull of seven years old, and tear down the altar of Baal that your father has, and cut down the wooden image that is beside it; and build an altar to the Lord your God on top of this rock in the proper arrangement, and take the second bull and offer a burnt sacrifice with the wood of the image which you shall cut down'" (Judges 6:25-26).

And this was how Israel was going to be saved from the Midianites? If Gideon furrowed his brow and wondered if the voice he heard was actually his late-night matzo bread snack instead of God, we can understand — and we can probably relate. God's voice seemed clear when it told Gideon he was going to save his country from the Midianites. But now this same voice appeared to give an odd step in that direction: tear down his father's idol. However, the lesson hidden within Gideon's first step stretches quite far.

Many times, the idols in our lives prevent us from walking in the complete victory that God desires for us to experience. If we have just one idol in our lives that we worship aside from God, we can be held in bondage. God desires to be first — and only — upon the throne of our lives. He felt so strongly about this fact, He made it the first of the Ten Commandments: "You shall have no other gods before Me" (Exodus 20:3).

The idols in our lives prevent us from walking in the complete victory that God desires for us to experience.

Gideon's first action demonstrated to his father and the people around them that serving any other god would no longer be acceptable. If they were going to triumph over the Midianites, God had to be seated in the highest place of their lives — and seated there alone.

Gideon's first step of obedience also shows how the Lord knows what groundwork we must lay in order to accomplish His greater plan for our lives. On the surface, tearing down an altar didn't seem like the first thing Gideon needed to do. How was this going to save Israel?

But this act set the tone for Gideon's leadership. He told the Lord he was going to do whatever He asked him to do, even if it seemed awkward. This was part of the Lord's process in preparing Gideon to be the leader who could lead Israel into battle against the Midianites and be successful through the method in which God wanted to win.

As soon as the Lord sees that we are going to be obedient, He recognizes that He now has a servant He can trust. And that's when God begins to empower us to accomplish His will. "But the Spirit of the Lord came upon Gideon" (v. 34).

Christ's Heart in You

1. Pray and ask God to reveal any idols you might have in your life that are preventing you from God's best for you.

2. In the past, how has God honored your decisions to be obedient no matter what the costs?

Pray: "Lord, help me to be obedient in everything I do as I follow Your will for my life."

<><

Day Three: Confirmation

If we received a phone call once a week from heaven, our struggle to know if the voice we heard was actually God would vanish. We would hang up with complete understanding that his instructions were clearly and undeniably His. There would be no need to worry, no need to agonize.

PursuingGod'sWord
Judges 6:36-40

But God doesn't use the phone — He prefers to impress things upon our hearts. We might hear the Lord speaking to us through His Holy Spirit or through His Word or through a trusted Christian brother or sister. However, since God doesn't usually appear in front of us for our own two eyes to see, processing instruction from the Lord is sometimes difficult.

Gideon, for all his strength and valor in battle, assumed his mantle of leadership quite timidly. God had sent an angel who spoke directly to Gideon about what he was to do. But Gideon still had his questions, his doubts, his fears. He wanted confirmation.

While Gideon's desire for confirmation is viewed by some as a weakness and inability to trust the Lord, it is anything but that. In his desire to serve the Lord, Gideon wanted to make sure that he was indeed following the Lord and not acting on a whim.

Oftentimes, Christians get a wild idea and think it's God. Without spending much time in prayer and counseling with other trusted believers, they rush off to do what they believe to be God's will without seeking Him on the matter. There are times when the Lord speaks directly to us and we must act immediately. But in a mission as grand as saving Israel from the Midianites, this was something that wasn't going to happen overnight; therefore, seeking the Lord for assurance that this indeed was His plan was wise by Gideon.

Gideon told the Lord, "If you will save Israel by my hand as You have said — look, I shall put a fleece of wool on the threshing floor; if there is dew on the fleece only, and it is dry on all the ground, then I shall know that You will save Israel by my hand, as you have said" (Judges 6:36-37). Verse 38 says, "And it was so." Gideon then asked for the opposite to happen, and God once again honored his request for confirmation.

Grounding ourselves in God's Word and asking Him to reveal His plans to us are wise.

As we listen for the Lord's direction for our lives, there is nothing wrong with seeking confirmation like Gideon. Grounding ourselves in God's Word and asking Him to reveal His plans to us are wise. David writes, "Show me Your ways, O Lord; teach me Your paths" (Psalm 25:4).

However, once God has revealed His ways to us, shown us His path, and confirmed it in our hearts, we must answer the call to serve. We must obey as we walk in full assurance that God will indeed be faithful to what He has promised us.

Christ's Heart in You

1. Whenever You receive what you believe to be God's leading in your life, what do you do to test it?

2. How do you typically react once something God spoke to you has been confirmed?

Pray: "Lord, show me Your ways so I may walk in them, obeying Your Word."

<><

Day Four: Committed to the Cause

Paul often described our relationship with God as a race or journey. He was also quick to point out that there is someone who wants to see you stalled in a ditch along the narrow path — the enemy. In Ephesians, Paul implores us to prepare each day for battle with the enemy, for our walk with Christ is anything but a casual stroll in the park.

The elements that comprise winning a battle are many: thoughtful plans, many supplies, effective weapons, superb leadership. However, one of the most important elements is that of dedicated and keen soldiers.

Gideon, who was now more than convinced that God wanted him to lead an army against the Midianites, knew what it would take to triumph in battle. As he began assembling the troops for Israel, God made it very clear to Gideon that He only wanted dedicated men.

Are we courageous, willing to forsake everything for the Lord?

Imagine Gideon's expression as he hears the Lord tell him, "The people who are with you are too many for Me to give the Midianites into their hands, lest Israel claim glory for itself against Me, saying, 'My own hand has saved me.' Now therefore, proclaim in the hearing of the people, saying, 'Whoever is fearful and afraid, let him turn and depart at once from Mount Gilead'" (Judges 7:2-3).

Of the 32,000 men who had assembled, 22,000 departed. At this point, it's safe to say that Gideon had relinquished all thoughts that he might actually know how God was going to give Israel victory.

But God wasn't done pruning the remaining 10,000. Gideon trimmed the troops again by asking all prospective soldiers to drink from the river. The men who put their face down in the water and drank without regard for their surroundings were dismissed. Only 300 men scooped the water into their hands, cautiously watching their environment.

And 300 men was all God needed to defeat a massive Midianite army. Man deals in numbers, size, and strength. God simply deals with the heart. He doesn't need a gigantic army to accomplish His goals — He just wants to use men and women who are dedicated to His cause, no matter what the cost.

If there has ever been a question in our minds as to whether God could use us to do something great, Gideon's story should settle our doubts. God called one man to lead and a paltry 300 men to follow in order to defeat a dominating army of that era. God began sifting through the volunteers looking for two things: courageous hearts and watchful people.

In our desire to be used by God, we, too, must inspect our own lives. Are we courageous, willing to forsake everything for the Lord? And are we ever watchful not to stumble, knowing that the enemy is lurking?

Jesus told His disciples, "For many are called, but few chosen" (Matthew 20:16). We are all called to serve the Lord the minute we profess Him to be our Lord and Savior. But are we daily renewing our minds and seeking to be more like Him so that we will be chosen?

Christ's Heart in You

1. Whenever God calls you to do something, what do you do to seek direction on how to move forward?

2. What things are obstacles to you in following God's direction for Your life?

Pray: "Lord, fill me with the courage to obey Your leading, especially when life seems difficult."

<><

Day Five: Pressing On

By the time the night of battle had arrived, Gideon was prepared, confident that God indeed was going to deliver the Midianites into his hands. Since the angel's visit to Gideon, he had seen a meal consumed by supernatural fire, two fleece requests answered, and heard a dream in the enemy's camp that foreshadowed Israel's victory. Gideon even had survived an angry mob of men who were upset over his tearing down of the altar of Baal.

PursuingGod'sWord
Judges 8:1-12

So, when it came time to blow their trumpets and shatter their pitchers, the 300 Israelites who were fighting with Gideon were just as confident. Their battle cry was nothing but affirmation that God was going to win the battle, not them: "The sword of the Lord and of Gideon!"

Without even lifting a sword in combat, the Israelites watched in the valley below as the Midianite camp broke into complete chaos. The

Midianites began fighting each other as they fled in sheer terror that they were about to be slaughtered by a massive army. There was no doubt that God had won the battle. So, was God through with Gideon?

> *He wants to continue refining us ... so we look more and more like His Son.*

Whenever God calls us to serve and inserts us into the thick of a battle, it's not a one-time occurrence. God doesn't use us once and discard us for the next up-and-coming saint. He wants to continue refining us through every battle — and victory — so we look more and more like His Son. In describing what God eventually wants to do with us, Paul writes, "For now we see in a mirror, dimly; but then face to face" (1 Corinthians 13:12).

After Gideon and his 300 men watched the Midianites flee in terror, they knew this was real. They understood that God's power was greater than anything they had ever seen. And their faith swelled. Even though they were tired, Gideon and his men pursued the retreating Midianites. (Judges 8:4) God wanted Gideon and his men to end the threat of attack for good, allowing His people to walk in true victory. Evidence of these soldiers' faith is apparent as they encountered Zebah and Zalmunna, two kings of Midian. These two kings carried with them 15,000 men, outnumbering Gideon's men 50 to 1. But Gideon's men pressed on and claimed victory, destroying more than 100,000 men total in this battle. No matter what the circumstances around them said, these men were so full of faith that they knew God was going to give them victory.

With each victory in battle, our faith grows as well. God isn't through with us — He is just getting started. Through these battles, we learn that we must press on even when we are tired and our flesh may not be up to the task at the moment. That's when we realize that it isn't our strength that's winning this battle for us — it's God's strength. He is the one carrying us. He is the one who will always lead us to victory.

Christ's Heart in You

1. In your relationship with God, are you preparing for the next battle or hoping He doesn't call?

2. When God wins a major victory in your life, how do you respond?

Pray: "Lord, empower me with Your strength to do the work of Your Kingdom, completely trusting in You for the victory."

<><

<u>Your Pursuit</u>

A Bold Witness

A Christian witness is an honest confession of what the Lord has done for us that may stir others to go and do likewise — to find the same Lord and His salvation.
— A. W. Tozer

Day One: Knowing the Promises

The Bible is full of promises for God's people. There are promises of hope and promises of joy for those who follow the Lord and serve Him faithfully. There are promises of destruction for those who reject Him. And there's the greatest promise of all: the promise of our salvation to all who believe upon the Lord, Jesus Christ.

PursuingGod'sWord
Psalm 119:105-112

As children of God, we must know His promises if we desire to witness effectively. A witness is one who has seen and heard, confirming the truth. Once we begin walking with the Lord, we, too, have seen and heard. In experiencing the wondrous love and mercy of our heavenly Father, our potential becomes great to witness powerfully God's salvation message.

John the Baptist knew the promises of God's Word. He knew that there was someone coming soon who was going to save the world from sin. And it was his knowledge of God's promises that helped enable him to deliver a powerful message to his followers. And they believed.

In foretelling of Jesus' coming, John the Baptist said, "I indeed baptize you with water unto repentance, but He who is coming after me is mightier than I, whose sandals I am not worthy to carry. He will baptize you with the Holy Spirit and fire" (Matthew 3:11).

All throughout the Old Testament, promises abounded of the Messiah. All the Jews waited in hope of His arrival. However, John the Baptist knew more than the simple fact that the Messiah was coming — he knew what the Messiah was going to do. What John the Baptist studied in the Word to be true, he shared it willingly with anyone who would listen.

David writes, "How sweet are Your words to my taste, sweeter than honey to my mouth! Through Your precepts I get understanding; therefore I hate every false way. Your word is a lamp to my feet and a light to my path" (Psalm 119: 103-105).

> *God's Word gives the direction we need, empowering us with the knowledge of His promises.*

God's Word gives the direction we need, empowering us with the knowledge of His promises. As we begin to follow and serve Him, we see the truth in these promises, giving us a witness that the world around us cannot deny. Whether it be in our words or actions, we must be willing to share these promises with the world.

A. W. Tozer writes, "A Christian witness is an honest confession of what the Lord has done for us that may stir others to go and do likewise — to find the same Lord and His salvation."

We must be diligent to study God's Word so that we know His promises while we experience them in our lives. In declaring the promises of God — promises which we have seen come to life in our own lives — the lost people of the world will hear the life-changing message of the Gospel.

Christ's Heart in You

1. In sharing with others God's plan of salvation, how do you use Scripture to support what you say?

2. How did Jesus use the Old Testament in His teachings?

Pray: "Lord, give me a deep love for Your Word and write it on my heart."

Day Two: Stepping Out in Faith

How willing are we to step out in faith for Jesus? Oftentimes we receive the opportunity to proclaim the name of Jesus in a bold way through looking at a dismal circumstance and trusting that God will change it despite its appearance. But are we bold enough to go forth

> **PursuingGod'sWord**
> Acts 3:1-10

with this when these situations arise in our lives?

There was nothing special in particular about this day as Peter and John headed to the temple for prayer. Just in the way they carried themselves, it was obvious a dramatic transformation had occurred in their lives. Peter, who had denied Christ three times before the rooster crowed, was now proclaiming the power of the resurrection to anyone who would listen — and to many who wouldn't.

As Peter and John neared the temple, a lame man sat outside the gates of the temple begging for money. The man had been begging there his whole life, and Peter undoubtedly had seen him more than once. But this morning, Peter decided that walking by again without giving him anything wouldn't suffice — it was time to step out in faith.

The beggar's healing ... set the entire temple to praising God.

"Then Peter said, 'Silver and gold I do not have, but what I do have I give you: In the name of Jesus Christ of Nazareth, rise up and walk'" (Acts 3:6). Peter said it. Peter believed it and so did the lame man.

"And he took him by the right hand and lifted him up, and immediately his feet and ankle bones received strength. So he, leaping up, stood and walked and entered the temple with them — walking, leaping, and praising God" (Acts 3:7-8).

The Bible mentions nothing about the state of the lame man's soul. Who knows if he believed Jesus was the Messiah? Who knows if he just sat outside the temple begging because he thought it was the best place to make money? But after Peter stepped out in faith, we know who bore witness to the lame man's soul.

No longer could the lame man deny the power of God, as he went walking and leaping and declaring God's name in the temple. The beggar's healing not only set him to dancing, but it set the entire temple to praising God. And it all started with Peter deciding to step out in faith in the midst of a seemingly hopeless situation.

Jesus told His disciples, "I say to you, if you have faith as a mustard seed, you will say to this mountain, 'Move from here to here,' and it will move; and nothing will be impossible for you" (Matthew 17:20).

So many times, the hardest step for us to take is the first one. We struggle to believe that something would actually happen if we did call upon the name of the Lord to change our circumstances — but He will. When God demonstrates His power through your faith, all those who see God's handiwork will not be able to deny Him any longer.

Christ's Heart in You

1. What do you do when God urges you to do something that would seem foolish to most people?

2. What has happened in the past when you have been willing to look foolish for Christ's sake?

Pray: "Lord, help me to step out in faith today in whatever You ask me to do."

<><

Day Three: In the Face of Persecution

A question has been directed toward us. We could say the answer everyone wants to hear, the answer that doesn't incite anger, or we can answer truthfully. It is a defining moment in our faith: Will we be known as someone who stands up for God in the midst of mockery?

PursuingGod'sWord
Acts 7:37-60

Stephen stood before the Sanhedrin council for accusations of blasphemy toward God. Despite the great signs and wonders Stephen was performing, a group of men in the synagogue was unhappy with a portion of his theology. They didn't like Stephen talking about Jesus all the time.

These men had accused Stephen of speaking against the Law. And a question was directed toward him: "The high priest said, 'Are these things so?'" (Acts 7:1).

What followed next was not a yes or no answer — Stephen instead delivered a powerful sermon that brought conviction to all who heard it. He didn't try to defend what he had preached, nor did he try to wriggle his way out of the blame. Stephen pleaded passionately for these men to see and understand the truth, hoping that they would respond by turning to the Lord.

Oftentimes when we are faced with a confrontation by someone in the world, we want to soften our stance so the Gospel doesn't sound so harsh. We want to sugarcoat the truth so that no one gets offended; but this isn't what Stephen tried to do.

Undoubtedly, Stephen could have talked his way through the convicting rhetoric and presented a Gospel that was acceptable to all who heard it. It may not have saved any lives, but it would have saved his. But what did Stephen say?

He wrapped up his short sermon with this: "You stiff-necked and uncircumcised in heart and ears! Which of the prophets did your fathers not persecute? And they killed those who foretold the coming of the Just One, of whom you now have become the betrayers and murderers, who have received the law by the direction of angels and have not kept it" (Acts 7:51-53).

We must not weaken the Gospel — we must present it powerfully and effectively, trusting that God will be the One who changes their hearts eventually.

As the Holy Spirit empowered Stephen to witness boldly, he held nothing back. We should be careful as we share the Gospel, exercising tact in our speech. But when the moment calls for it, we must not weaken the Gospel — we must present it powerfully and effectively, trusting that God will be the One who eventually changes their hearts.

Oswald Chambers explains why we can have boldness in the midst of persecution: "The things we try to avoid and fight against — tribulation, suffering, and persecution — are the very things that produce abundant joy in us. 'We are more than conquerors through Him' 'in all these things'; not in spite of them, but in the midst of them. A saint doesn't know the joy of the Lord in spite of tribulation, but because of it."

We must be His servants, faithful to deliver the message whenever — and however — it must be delivered. And God will be responsible for changing hearts.

Christ's Heart in You

1. How do you react in the face of persecution for your faith in Christ?

2. When you know other people will be strongly opposed to the Gospel, how do you share the Gospel message?

Pray: "Lord, empower me through Your Holy Spirit to boldly share Your love in the midst of persecution."

<><

Day Four: Listening to the Holy Spirit

Deep down in our hearts, we know it is the Lord. His soft, gentle voice is urging us to do something . . . and we're not quite sure we want to do it. What God is asking us to do seems a little bit silly or out of the ordinary. But whether we are comfortable with what He is telling us, we know we need to obey.

Pursuing**God'sWord**
Acts 8:26-40

Philip was beginning to experience great growth in his ministry. As he served the Lord and was willing to communicate the heart of God to all who would listen, amazing signs and wonders followed Philip. He was casting out demons and healing lame and paralyzed people. And people were following him.

The Holy Spirit is our guide, leading us into the places where God desires us to be.

So, we can imagine that when Philip heard the Holy Spirit leading him elsewhere — down a desert road leading to Gaza — that he was somewhat perplexed. (Acts 8:26) Why would the Lord take him out of a place of great impact? How could he make as many strides for the Kingdom of God on this road?

Many times we think of being bold in our witness as stepping into a situation where the Gospel may not be well-received. However, being bold in our witness also means surrendering ourselves to Him in such a way that wherever He calls us, whenever He calls us, we will be obedient and go. This is what Philip did.

The boldness that came for Philip in his encounter with the Ethiopian eunuch started long before he arrived alongside the man's chariot — it started when Philip began walking down that long desert road.

In our walk with the Lord, we must be attentive to the Holy Spirit speaking to us. That is the beginning of obedience. Before we ever can act according to God's will, we must get a clear picture of what He wants us to do. For Philip, that picture started with walking down a desert road with no promise of what he would find there.

But what he found was an opportunity to share Christ with a hungry man, a man who could influence an entire nation. The Ethiopian eunuch was so excited about being baptized that they stopped near some water and Philip baptized him. "And Philip said, 'If you believe with all your heart, you may [be baptized].' And he answered and said, 'I believe that Jesus Christ is the Son of God'" (Acts 8:37).

The Holy Spirit is our guide, leading us into the places where God desires us to be. Jesus said, "When the Helper comes, whom I send to you from the Father, that is the Spirit of truth who proceeds from the Father, He will testify about Me, and you will testify also, because you have been with Me from the beginning" (John 15:26-27).

As we listen to the voice of the Holy Spirit in our lives, we will have the opportunity to be used in ways that we never imagined, ways that can change an entire nation on a desert road.

Christ's Heart in You

1. How do you react when God calls you to do something entirely against the norm?

2. Do you live your life in daily expectancy to hear the voice of the Holy Spirit? Why or why not?

Pray: "Lord, prepare my heart to hear the Holy Spirit today and give me the courage to be obedient."

<><

Day Five: When It's Not Convenient

We may recognize an opportunity to share the Gospel with someone, but we just don't feel like it. Maybe it's late or we're supposed to be somewhere shortly, so we don't respond. We assume the opportunity will arise later if the Lord really wants us to talk to that person and go on with our lives. We begin to walk away, and the Lord is still tugging at our hearts to speak to them.

> **PursuingGod'sWord**
> Acts 16:25-34

Sitting chained in a prison cell with Silas, Paul probably thought it best to leave out times such as these in recruiting others to serve the Lord in the capacity of a missionary. Unable to write or talk with the other prisoners, Paul resorted to spreading the Gospel with Silas through song. As the two began to sing of the wonders of their Lord, the foundations of the prison began to shake — and it shook them loose.

As the prisoners were freed by the shaking of the earth, all the jailer could imagine was a wild jailbreak with himself left to pay the consequences of it happening upon his watch. Paul and Silas were undoubtedly caught up in the moment, rejoicing that the Lord had somehow provided a way out of this unjust situation for them. What a relief to know that the God of the universe was looking out for them!

But as freedom rang in their hearts, Paul and Silas saw one man still imprisoned — the jailer. At midnight, the jailer had been asleep before the shaking of the jail and opening of the jail cells awoke him. He arose to discover the horror of all the jail cells being open. He knew that rebuke from his superiors was inevitable even though it was beyond his control. Shame would be heaped upon his head — and they might kill him for acting irresponsibly.

> *Part of being a bold witness means sacrificing our desires for the moment in an effort to make an eternal impact.*

Yet Paul forgot about his open invitation to physical freedom and turned his attention toward bringing eternal freedom to a man held in spiritual bondage. This was not the ideal time to share the Gospel with the jailer, but it was evident to Paul that the dire situation called for action.

"He drew his sword and was about to kill himself, supposing that the prisoners had escaped. But Paul cried out with a loud voice, 'Do not harm yourself, for we are all here!' … [the jailer then] said, 'Sirs, what must I do to be saved?' (Acts 16:27-30).

Before the night was over, not only was the jailer saved, but so was his entire family. And by the next morning, so was his life, as the magistrates realized what a terrible injustice had been performed against Paul and Silas, two Roman citizens.

Part of being a bold witness means sacrificing our desires for the moment in an effort to make an eternal impact. When we find ourselves willing to lay aside our lives for just a moment to reach someone who is struggling or hungry for the Gospel, we discover a fountain of joy in what God can do through us.

Christ's Heart in You

1. How willing are you to serve God, even when it is extremely inconvenient or awkward?

2. How has God moved through you in the past when you've made such sacrifices?

Pray: "Lord, I want to obey You no matter how inconvenient or how costly."

Your Pursuit

Cultivating Humility

Let this be thy whole endeavor, this thy prayer, this thy desire, — that thou mayest be stripped of all selfishness, and with entire simplicity follow Jesus only.
— Thomas a Kempis

Day One: The Perils of Pride

PursuingGod'sWord
James 4:1-10

The little 5-year-old stood in shock at the words of his mother. "We're so proud of what you've done," she said in an effort to encourage her son and show him approval. But the little boy would have none of it: he learned in Sunday School that he didn't want to be near the word "proud." He quickly shot back, "Mom, we're not supposed to be proud."

Although the boy misunderstood the word's intention, one concept had been ingrained in his mind at an early age — pride was wrong.

As we step back and assess our own lives, pride appears to be a sin that we aren't too concerned about addressing. And why bother? Sometimes it can be glaring to others, but more often than not it's tucked neatly away within the dark recesses of our hearts.

However, if we knew the severity with which God views pride in our hearts, we would make an immediate effort to cleanse our heart from the cancer that robs us of a greater understanding of God's glory. Pride isn't a sin that simply self-promotes; pride accomplishes its task of self-promotion at the expense of everyone around, including God.

In James, we learn one important truth about a man full of pride: "God sets Himself against the proud, but He shows favor to the humble" (James 4:6, NLT). That alone should send us scurrying for search lights that can expose the darkness of pride in our own lives. But that's only part of what pride can bring.

In Proverbs, King Solomon warns us of the eventual fruits of pride

49

in our lives. We're informed that it brings about shame (Prov. 11:2), strife (13:10), and destruction (16:18).

Pride accomplishes its task of self-promotion at the expense of everyone around, including God.

Through these passages, we understand that even though pride may remain hidden in our hearts, the fruits of pride will manifest themselves through shame, contention, and destruction. How many times have we seen the openly arrogant fall? No matter how much power, fame, favor, or security one has, the pride in one's heart will eventually be brought to light.

As believers, we desire favor with God, and that favor comes about through extinguishing our pride and developing a heart of humility. In the book *A Serious Call*, William Law describes true humility: "Humility does not consist in having a worse opinion of ourselves than we deserve, or in abasing ourselves lower than we really are. But as all virtue is founded in truth, so humility is founded in a true and just sense of our weakness, misery, and sin. He that rightly feels and lives in this sense of his condition lives in humility."

When we understand the perils of pride, surely we will begin striving for a heart of humility, one that fully understands where it stands in relationship to our heavenly Father.

Christ's Heart in You

1. How do you react when you recognize an area of pride in your life?

2. Ask some friends or your spouse to be willing to point out patterns of pride in your life and then pray about them.

Pray: "Lord, give me the same view of pride as You have and help me to see humility as I seek You."

<><

Day Two: Recognizing God's Greatness

In those moments when our paradigm of life shifts, we begin to see that what we once thought to be great isn't — or what we thought wasn't, in fact, is.

PursuingGod'sWord
Exodus 34:29-34

From the outside, the house didn't appear like much. Day after day, Larry drove by this one house that was a good distance from the road. He often wondered who lived there, somewhat pitying them for the very moderate decor. "That house could look so nice," Larry thought to himself.

One afternoon on his way home from work, Larry's car blew out a tire as it came to a stop just in front of the house that always captured his attention. Just as Larry was getting prepared to change his tire, the owner of the house was pulling into the driveway when he noticed Larry. He then quickly pulled his car into the driveway and raced out to help Larry. After a few minutes of wrestling with the tire and getting it fixed, the man invited Larry into his home to wash his hands and get something to drink. Curious about the home, Larry accepted.

When we begin to recognize the greatness of God, we begin to understand what true humility is all about.

However, what Larry saw inside totally changed his image of the home forever. Although the house looked bland from a distance, majestic marble columns appeared in place of what Larry believed to be wood. Beautiful inscriptions and detailed images decorated the stone surrounding the home, and the inside was even more grand. Larry was dumbfounded.

As Larry later drove away, his feelings suddenly changed. Instead of feeling sorry for the man, he began to feel sorry for himself — sorry that he had ever thought such a thing, and sorry that his house was nothing as wonderful as the man's home.

When we begin to recognize the greatness of God, we begin to understand what true humility is all about. His love for us, His character, His nature — it's more incredible than we could ever think about being. Yet many of us remain at a distance from God, unable to see the fullness of His glory, patting ourselves on the back about how great we believe ourselves to be.

Although Moses lived in awe of God, his understanding of God's glory was increased after spending over a month on the mountain with the Lord. While Moses was there, God had revealed His glory to His faithful servant that left a visible mark on Moses.

"Now it was so, when Moses came down from Mount Sinai . . . that Moses did not know that the skin of his face shone while he talked with Him" (Exodus 34:29). Moses' face was so bright that he had to put a veil on his face so the children of Israel could look at him.

From that moment forth, there was no second-guessing for Moses.

He had seen first-hand the wonders of God and his life would be forever changed.

In our efforts to develop a humble heart, we must see ourselves in light of who God really is. His majesty, His glory, His beauty — we pale in comparison to the ultimate Light. And when this truth finds its way into our hearts, pride must find another home.

My effort to praise?

Christ's Heart in You

1. What words come to mind when you see God's glory before you?

2. How does your heart change when you realize God at work in your life in an "impossible" situation?

Pray: "Lord, remind me of your glory each day to help me to keep you in perspective of who I am."

<><

Day Three: Adjusting Our Self-View

After graduating from college with a business degree, the young man postponed his job search for a few months. He decided he needed to set out on a road trip across America to "find himself."

PursuingGod'sWord
Psalm 139:19-24

There were many things in life he knew he could become or many things his parents wanted him to become, but before he went down any of those avenues, he wanted to find out who he really was. Living outside of the comfortable boundaries everyone had constructed for him, the young man was free to become who he really was, not who everyone else had decided he would be.

In our efforts to develop a humble heart, we must be diligent to discover who we really are, ignoring the lies of the enemy that have so penetrated our hearts along the way. Thinking we are great or that God desires to hide Himself from us are two ways the enemy tries to trick us into hardening our hearts and nurturing an attitude of pride.

Blaise Pascal once wrote, "Knowing God without knowing our own wretchedness makes for pride. Knowing our own wretchedness without knowing God makes for despair. Knowing Jesus Christ strikes the balance because He shows us both God and our own wretchedness."

David had acquired an understanding for how a humble heart should work. If it was bent on allowing God to transform it, revealing his true self, it indeed would remain humble. He wrote, "Search me, O God, and know my heart; try me, and know my anxieties; and see if there is any wicked way in me, and lead me in the way everlasting" (Psalm 139:23-24).

> *We must discover who we really are in light of God.*

As we discover who we are in light of God's greatness, we see just how far we really are from who we should be — and it keeps us humble.

Paul was already there. Even though he had experienced an incredible outpouring of God's grace, he maintained the correct view of himself: one that understood God's love for him, yet one that understood his wretchedness on earth. He writes, "For now we see in a mirror, dimly, but then face to face. Now I know in part, but then I shall know just as I also am known" (1 Corinthians 13:12).

God doesn't want to crush us with His power; instead, He wants to show us His beauty and how we can become all that He has created us to be. And only a correct self-view — one that understands how weak and wretched we are, yet how God still completely loves us — will allow us to walk in a constant state of humility.

Christ's Heart in You

1. How often are you willing to ask God to search your heart?

2. How can an adjusted view of yourself change your heart?

Pray: "Lord, show me who I am in light of You and show me how to walk in humility."

<><

Day Four: Benefits of a Humble Heart

To the members of the congregation, the preacher standing behind the pulpit was merely a talking head. Sunday after Sunday, the preacher delivered powerful sermon after powerful sermon. But

PursuingGod'sWord
Romans 12:3-8

Sunday after Sunday, the people filed out more discouraged than when they entered. It seemed to the people that the pastor already had everything figured out in his walk with the Lord and that his sermons were designed to instruct the poor, directionless people in the audience. A pretentious heart is unable to communicate effectively, for in its pretentious state is lost the trait of humility.

Jesus' words are our roadmap to survival and success.

Despite all the glory that eventually was and still is bestowed upon the Son of God, Jesus was anything but pretentious. His amazing heart of humility was revealed constantly to his disciples or the hungry crowd who followed him around. He spoke with authority, not condemnation. While His authority rested in His relationship with God, His authority also came in the form of experience: Jesus really had walked a mile in these people's sandals.

Praying on His face in the Garden of Gethsemane, Jesus told His disciples, "Watch and pray, lest you enter into temptation. The spirit indeed is willing, but the flesh is weak" (Matthew 26:41).

And there in the dark hours before His trial and crucifixion, Jesus reveals the true state of His heart. He was determined to be obedient, but He wasn't full of pride. As the weight of the impending events began to weigh heavily upon Him, Jesus admitted His weakness to His disciples, who likewise were struggling, albeit simply to stay awake. But this wasn't easy for Jesus, nor did He make any claims that it would be.

We also see that Jesus was tempted just as we are, withstanding the attacks of the enemy when He was in the desert for 40 days fasting. He didn't blow off the devil with some supernatural power and then come back to us and say "resist temptation." When Jesus later told us to pray for God to "not lead us into temptation but deliver us from the evil one" (Matthew 6:13), His authority comes thundering through. We realize that this Man has indeed gone where we are going, surviving unscathed. Now, His words are our roadmap to survival and success.

In our efforts to encourage fellow believers in their relationships with God, a pretentious heart — one full of pride — cannot effectively show others the way home. Others are left frustrated, wondering if they will ever be able to break free of the bondage they are in or if they will ever conquer their weakness.

Jesus didn't try to trick anyone, and neither should we. In our desire to develop a heart of humility, we will find quickly that not only will we benefit with a healthier relationship with our heavenly Father, but others will benefit too when they see they aren't alone in their struggles.

Christ's Heart in You

1. How do you portray yourself in sharing with other believers? Do you ask them questions about how they handle certain issues in their relationship with God?

2. How often do you share your personal struggles with others?

Pray: "Lord, give me boldness to share with others when I am hurting or weak, realizing through my weakness You bring Your strength."

<><

Day Five: Staying Humble

One event that will one day come to pass is the humbling of all mankind. Eventually, every knee will bow and confess that Jesus Christ is indeed Lord. (Philippians 2:10) In our desire to obtain a spirit of humility, we sometimes grow frustrated, thinking that it's a special gift that God gives some people but not everyone. Despite our best efforts, we grow weary of trying to shake our pride. But throughout the Scripture, we begin understanding that this state of humility isn't something that God bestows upon certain people, but it's an attitude of the heart God desires us all to have.

> **PursuingGod'sWord**
> Micah 6:1-8

Looking for direction, Israel gets instruction from God through the prophet Micah: "He has shown you, O man, what is good; and what does the Lord require of you but to do justly, to love mercy, and to walk humbly with your God" (Micah 6:8). The Lord desired for the people of Israel to walk in humility.

But how do we walk consistently in a state of humility? Peter, who is often synonymous with his character flaw of pride when he was a disciple, eventually discovered the secret to walking in humility. He shares it with us in one of his letters: "Therefore humble yourselves under the mighty hand of God, that He may exalt you in due time, casting all your care upon Him, for He cares for you" (1 Peter 5:6-7).

The way to humble ourselves should now become synonymous with Peter's addendum: cast your care upon the Lord. But how does this keep us humble?

Through maintaining a proper perspective on our lives and recognizing God's gracious hand on us, we begin to see just how helpless we are when we are flailing through life on our own. We begin to see that we indeed are *not* self-sufficient. We begin to realize our inability to withstand life's trials and temptations. We begin to see that we need Him.

He wants us to run to Him with the understanding that He truly is our Savior.

And that's what God wants! He wants us to run to Him with the understanding that He truly is our Savior. With this in mind, there is no place for pride in our hearts. When we understand how much we need to give Him our cares, we begin to walk in the humility that He desires for us to walk in — and He can begin to use us in ways never possible before.

In the book *Seeking the Face of God*, author Gary L. Thomas explains how walking in humility forever transforms our outlook on our own lives as well as the lives of others: "Spiritual maturity means we hold ourselves to a high standard while being gracious toward others. When we know we have been forgiven and when we're not cherishing sin in our hearts, it is not difficult to offer a word of healing and grace to others who are struggling."

In our desire to walk in humility, let us lay hold of God's truth for our lives, understanding that we need Him more than anything in this world.

Christ's Heart in You

1. Is "casting your cares" upon God a regular occurrence in your life? Why or why not?

2. How do you deal with feelings of self-sufficiency when you recognize them in your life?

Pray: "Lord, help me to realize my need for You in every moment of my life."

<><

Your Pursuit

Going the Distance

---

*The readiest way to escape from our sufferings is
to be willing they should endure as long as God pleases.*
— John Wesley

Day One: Withstanding Weariness

As he glared back across the desert, Elijah stumbled again. He couldn't get to the middle of nowhere fast enough. Running from Queen Jezebel was tiring, but continuous glancing over his shoulder only seemed to make matters worse for Elijah.

| PursuingGod'sWord |
| Psalm 18 |

Finally, distraught and out of breath, Elijah fell asleep under a broom tree. It's hard to believe that this exhausted man who now feared for his life was the same man who just called down fire from heaven and brought judgment upon the prophets of Baal. How quickly he forgot the victory.

We are all prone to wear down after an intense battle. The exhaustion of standing up to the enemy can be taxing for even the strongest man or woman of God. We even forget how He has delivered us from our most dire circumstances. However, God is faithful to bring us rest, restoring us to do His work.

"Then as [Elijah] lay and slept under a broom tree, suddenly an angel touched him, and said to him, 'Arise and eat.' Then he looked, and there by his head was a cake baked on coals, and a jar of water. So he ate and drank, and lay down again. And the angel of the Lord came back the second time, and touched him, and said, 'Arise and eat, because the journey is too great for you.' So he arose, and ate and drank; and he went in the strength of that food forty days and forty nights as far as Horeb, the mountain of God" (1 Kings 19:5-8).

At times, our stubborn wills believe that we can endure the

59

journey — this great journey — all on our own. But we quickly learn otherwise. We need God to be our strength.

If we are to go the distance with the Lord, we must learn to handle weariness in our walk with Him.

King David writes: "The Lord is my rock and my fortress and my deliverer; my God, my strength, in whom I will trust; my shield and the horn of my salvation, my stronghold" (Psalm 18:2).

If we are to go the distance with the Lord, we must learn to handle weariness in our walk with Him whenever we encounter it. Weariness is not a sign of weakness; rather, it's a sign that we are pouring ourselves out unto the Lord. But when we are spent and these times of weariness come, neither can we attempt to rely on our own strength nor can we give up.

Going the distance with the Lord is never easy. There are days when even the strongest of believers have experienced enough of life's hard knocks and unjust treatment. But quitting isn't a viable option.

In our desire to go the distance with the Lord, walking out the teachings of Jesus in our every-day lives, we must learn from another weary saint, Elijah. We must draw upon God's strength to press on when we are weary, for He leads us to His mountain where we hear His instruction for our lives in a still small voice.

Christ's Heart in You

1. How do you respond to weariness in your life?

2. How can you ensure that you aren't trying to make it through life on your own strength?

Pray: "Lord, give me a heart that leans on You and nothing else."

Day Two: Getting over Guilt

For all the enemy's wiles, his most twisted weapon might be his urging us to sin and then heaping guilt upon our heads in the aftermath. We begin to experience feelings of unworthiness as we come to

PursuingGod'sWord
Psalm 51

the realization that we have indeed sinned against God. Guilt and shame take over our lives, and we begin to feel worthless before our King.

King David wasn't perfect — in fact, he was quite far from perfection. His mistakes cost him dearly and his sin cost him more than he ever could make up for. However, David, who was called a man after God's own heart (Acts 13:22), understood God's amazing heart of forgiveness. And it was during his most depressing times that God began to do the work of a lifetime in him.

David's sin with Bathsheba was deplorable. Why would he do such a thing? Did he not think through the consequences that would befall such an action? To commit adultery and then have the woman's husband murdered in battle all to cover up his sin — the guilt and shame only seemed to double its weight upon the head of David.

Wallowing in our shame with feelings of unworthiness is not what God intended.

It was during this mournful period that David penned some of his most heartfelt psalms — psalms that strike a chord in the hearts of all believers who feel as though they have let God down and will never be restored.

David writes, "Purge me with hyssop, and I shall be clean; wash me, and I shall be whiter than snow. . . . Create in me a clean heart, O God, and renew a steadfast spirit within me. Do not cast me away from Your presence, and do not take Your Holy Spirit from me" (Psalm 51:7, 10-11)

Before the Lord, David held nothing back. There was no use hiding under the guilt and shame any longer. David wanted to be cleansed, freed, released. Trying to endure life and bear the weight of his guilt was more than David could handle. He had to turn it over to the Lord.

As soon as Bathsheba bore David's son, David's first test came: Would he indeed turn everything over to the Lord? Would the burden and shame be lifted? David fasted furiously, petitioning God to have mercy and spare the child. But there were consequences for the sinful actions of David, something we oftentimes like to ignore in addressing issues of sin in our lives. And the child died soon after birth.

As soon as the baby died, David quit mourning, ceased fasting, and returned to ruling the kingdom. His servants thought him heartless, but David understood God's heart of forgiveness.

If we truly desire to go the distance with the Lord, we must come to an understanding of what His grace, love, and forgiveness are all about. Wallowing in our shame with feelings of unworthiness is not what God intended for our lives. When we stumble, we must get up and press on. We have to assume responsibility for our mistakes, understanding that there will be consequences. However, we must follow David's lead, returning to God's presence so He can purify us again.

"The sacrifices of God are a broken spirit, a broken and a contrite heart — these, O God, You will not despise" (Psalm 51:17).

Christ's Heart in You

1. What is your typical response to guilt in your life?

2. How have you seen God's grace win out over feelings of unworthiness?

Pray: "Lord, help me to realize that Your grace is sufficient for me."

<><

Day Three: Refusing to Bow

The gigantic golden image towered over the people of Babylon. They were amazed at the beauty of such an idol, drawn to it as if it indeed was all powerful. Then, King Nebuchadnezzar issued a decree: When the music plays, everyone must bow down and worship the idol or else be thrown into the fiery furnace.

Pursuing God's Word
Daniel 3:8-18

As we desire to go the distance with the Lord, we must be determined to go His way.

The incessant drone of the world attacks our thoughts daily. "Come join us," the voices say without regard to the inevitable consequences of following them. "Look what we have! Isn't it beautiful?!"

Despite our best efforts to hold our ground, the world desires for us to conform to its ways, to join them in their hollow pursuit of happiness and peace. The world's way appears easy, paved with good intentions yet leading to the middle of nowhere. God's way looks tough, almost uninviting. If it weren't for the prize at the end, it might make us wonder why we ever chose such a difficult path.

But we can see the prize that awaits us at the end of our earthly journey of faithfulness to God. We see that He wants to crown us and make us heirs to His throne. Suddenly, the struggles and the difficulties appear possible to endure, for forsaking God for the way of the world seems less and less attractive. Why would we ever want to conform?

Shadrach, Meshach, and Abed-Nego were asking themselves the same question when the officials came calling. These three men were under interrogation for their refusal to bow down to the giant idol when the music played. These three men weren't going to conform to the world.

King Nebuchadnezzar wanted to give them another chance, thinking maybe they misunderstood the directive. He then clearly threatened them again, asking in all his vanity, "And who is the god who will deliver you from my hands?"

"Shadrach, Meshach, and Abed-Nego answered and said to the king, 'O Nebuchadnezzar, we have no need to answer you in this matter. If that is the case, our God whom we serve is able to deliver us from the burning fiery furnace, and He will deliver us from your hand, O king. But if not, let it be known to you, O king, that we do not serve your gods, nor will we worship the gold image which you have set up'" (Daniel 3:16-18).

Job, who endured great heartache for the Lord, encountered the same type of pressure from his so-called friends who wanted him to give up on God. But Job knew conforming wasn't the answer. He said, "All the days of my hard service, I will wait, till my change comes" (Job 14:14).

As we desire to go the distance with the Lord, we must be determined to go His way. There are no other paths. We've seen what the world has to offer and it's all a façade. God's way, however, has depth. It's real and eternal. And it's the only way we find worthy of conforming to.

Christ's Heart in You

1. What areas of life seem to have a tendency to draw you away from God?

2. How do you stand up to things that test your commitment to God?

Pray: "Lord, help me to stand strong against worldly temptations."

<><

Day Four: Standing Up for Christ

The accusations were ludicrous. Stephen, a heretic? The men in power in the synagogue thought so, and that seemed to be all that mattered. All of a sudden, all the signs and wonders that were follow-

PursuingGod'sWord
Luke 21:7-19

ing Stephen's ministry were forgotten. They apparently lent no credibility to the fact that Stephen indeed was doing the will of his heavenly Father. The council would hear nothing of it. All they were interested in was stopping his ministry that propagated the belief that Jesus was the Son of God, undermining their authority within the religious community.

Instead of concocting a way to avenge our persecutors, we must recognize this as an opportunity to show them Christ.

As we commit to going the distance with the Lord, sticking with His ways and His principles through every trying circumstance, we must know that persecution is coming. We must also know that this is an opportunity to shine for Christ.

Jesus warned His disciples of such troubling days ahead. He said, "They will lay their hands on you and persecute you, delivering you up to the synagogues and prisons. You will be brought before kings and rulers for My name's sake. But it will turn out for you as an occasion for testimony. Therefore settle it in your hearts not to meditate beforehand on what you will answer; for I will give you a mouth and wisdom which all your adversaries will not be able to contradict or resist" (Luke 21:12-15).

There may have been days in the past when you have had to endure something for the Lord. Or you may be going through a time of persecution for your faith now. It may not be one that finds us in prison, but the world around us will certainly put us on trial for what we believe.

Perhaps Stephen knew that he would soon be standing before a religious council defending his faith, but he certainly didn't prepare for what rolled off his tongue in response to their accusations. Instead of defending himself, Stephen simply presented the Gospel, reiterating why he believed what he did.

Just like Jesus said that persecution would be an opportunity for us to testify of how great He is, Stephen delivered. He took their inevitable fatal stoning with dignity, staring into heaven and asking for their forgiveness from the heavenly Father. Down to his dying words, Stephen was a shining testimony.

"And they stoned Stephen as he was calling on God and saying, 'Lord Jesus, receive my spirit.' Then he knelt down and cried out with a loud voice, 'Lord, do not charge them with this sin.' And when he had said this, he fell asleep" (Acts 7:59-60).

Instead of concocting a way to avenge our persecutors, we must recognize this as an opportunity to show them Christ. As we determine to go the distance in serving God here on earth, these opportunities will arise in our lives more frequently–and more frequently, we can glorify and honor Him, pointing the world around us to Christ.

Christ's Heart in You

1. How do you handle criticism of the Gospel when in the presence of unbelievers?

2. What does Jesus tell us to do when we're attacked over the Gospel for which we live?

Pray: "Lord, help me to rely upon You for wisdom to speak the truth when others question the Gospel."

Day Five: Battling to Victory

If Paul had decided to break away and swim from his captors, no one would have blamed him. After all, everyone knew he didn't deserve to be taken captive. If preaching the Gospel was indeed a crime, Paul deserved his prison sentence — but it wasn't and he didn't. Nevertheless, Paul, imprisoned by the Romans, decided not to run from the centurion guards.

PursuingGod'sWord
1 Corinthians 9:24-27

Nearing the end of his ministry, Paul probably grew weary as he took the Gospel message abroad. As he grew older, the endless travel couldn't have been good for his health — neither could have the imprisonment been good for him. But on this day when he could've made the decision to attempt to escape his captors, there was no decision to be made: Paul made his decision a long time before this moment. He had determined, with the help of the Holy Spirit, that he never wanted to do anything that contradicted what he said he believed.

So, Paul complied with the prison guards on the island of Malta following the shipwreck — and God used him. First, Paul survived a scare when a snake bit him but did no harm. All the prisoners and guards began believing that maybe there was something to this man and his message. Then Publius, the highest ranking Roman official on the island, had a sick father. Paul offered to pray for him, and God healed Publius' father. Many other sick people began coming to Paul for prayer, and they too were healed.

In going the distance with the Lord, we must establish in our hearts what we confess with our mouths.

For Paul, this lifestyle of which he passionately preached was not just lofty words — it was, in fact, the way he lived his life. He writes, "Do you not know that those who run in a race all run, but one receives the prize? Run in such a way that you may obtain it. ... I discipline my body and bring it into subjection, lest, when I have preached to others, I myself should become disqualified" (1 Corinthians 9:24, 27).

In going the distance with the Lord, we must establish in our hearts what we confess with our mouths. When the moment of decision comes, are we going to run from trouble or run to victory? Do we fully trust that our Lord and Savior is going to deliver us and bring glory to Himself as He has promised to do?

People always live up to their beliefs, Christian or not. Rest assured, the tests will come and we will be faced with making a decision. Paul's testimony speaks for what he truly believed. This man decided he was going to go the distance with the Lord. Whether it was facing an angry crowd or imprisonment or persecution, Paul was committed to the Lord no matter what it cost him.

If we are going to be a people who are committed to going the distance, we too must show the world that our walk is real, that our lives are genuine. We must demonstrate that going the distance isn't a lofty goal, but rather it's an achievement that can be obtained when we commit our hearts and ways to Him on a daily basis.

Christ's Heart in You

1. What are some areas in your own life where you can deepen your commitment to God?

2. How does your lifestyle match your belief in God?

Pray: "Lord, help me through Your Holy Spirit to walk out what I believe, giving myself to Your ways each day."

<><

Your Pursuit

Following God

Trust the past to God's mercy, the present to God's love and the future to God's providence.
— St. Augustine

Day One: The Call

Sometimes we hear God's call in a faint voice, a whisper, or a quiet moment sitting still before Him. Other times, His voice comes thundering to us through a fellow brother or sister in Christ. Or we might see Him speaking to us through our circumstances. But He is speaking.

PursuingGod'sWord
Matthew 4:18-22

Each time we hear the Lord speak to us, there's one specific purpose for it all. He wants us to keep following Him — something we can't do if we never hear Him speak.

When God first speaks to us and we know it's Him, our hearts leap. The King of the universe wants to commune with us; He wants us to follow Him. And the first time He speaks, we become excited about the prospect of spending an eternity getting to know Him.

There was Peter drawing up his nets on the shore of the sea of Galilee when God called him to a relationship. For the rugged fisherman, the fact that this man Jesus knew his name was exciting enough. But the prospect of exchanging the monotonous life of fishing for a life of adventure with Jesus sparked Peter to an instant response. "Then [Jesus] said to them, 'Follow Me, and I will make you fishers of men.' They immediately left their nets and followed Him" (Matthew 4:19-20).

God has called us all into a relationship with Him. However, it's up to us to continue on after Him once the call has been issued. A life of unknown excitement awaits — it awaits with the ultimate tour guide on the ride of a lifetime.

In the book *The Sacred Romance*, co-author Brent Curtis writes of how God calls us to Him and we sense it: "Someone or something has romanced us from the beginning with creekside singers and pastel sunset with the austere majesty of snowcapped mountains and the poignant flames of autumn colors telling us of something — or someone — leaving

God has called us all into a relationship with Him.

with a promise to return. These things can, in an unguarded moment, bring us to our knees with longing for this something or someone who is lost; someone or something only our heart recognizes."

God doesn't ever force us to do something against our wills. In His perfect timing, our hearts recognize the Lord's call. We know of the perilous roads and uncertain twists and turns. Deep down, we also know that this is what we really want and that this life of mundane punching th clock for Jesus is nothing more than the acknowledgment of His plan while we stick behind and continue packing for a trip we are too scared t take.

Whether we are just beginning the first leg of this adventure or coming into the homestretch, God is still calling. He forever remains out on the trail of His glorious journey, directing us to His side along the way. And we won't be disappointed in the journey — or His ultimate destination for our lives.

Christ's Heart in You

1. How have you responded to God's leading in your past? Your present?

2. How would you characterize the direction you have for your life?

Pray: "Lord, show me Your direction for my life and help me to be courageous enough to obey."

<><

Day Two: His Direction

In our efforts to follow the Lord, we must understand that our signing up for the trip doesn't include a detailed map. The final destination is known: a growing, thriving intimate relationship with the heaven ly Father that transforms us into the person He created us to be. And the

PursuingGod'sWor
Mark 8:34-38

hope and anticipation of reaching that place should quiet the anxiety in our hearts.

It's Saturday afternoon and the kids are complaining, whining, fighting. So, in an effort to restore a little happiness to the upset children, the father decides a little ice cream might do the trick. "Come on, kids," he says. "Everybody get your shoes on. We're going out."

For a moment, everything stops — the crying, the fighting, the complaining. Then the silence is broken by the question of all questions: "Where are we going, dad?"

To tell them would ruin the surprise, but to mistakenly believe that they're going to agreeably get into the minivan and follow dad would ruin the father's day. So, he tells them. "We're going to get ice cream," he says. Instead of hearing more complaining, more whining, more fighting, the only sounds that come from the children's rooms are the pitter patter of little feet scurrying about in search of their shoes speckled with squeals of delight.

No itinerary.
No schedule.
No road map.
He just tells
us where
we're going.

None of the kids care what roads their father intends to maneuver down, nor do they care how long it's going to take. The promise of ice cream is good enough for them, and they'll behave as long as it takes for them to get some.

If only we were that agreeable when God beckons us to follow Him. Jesus told His disciples, "Whoever desires to come after Me, let him deny himself, and take up his cross, and follow Me" (Mark 8:34).

No itinerary. No schedule. No road map. He just tells us where we're going.

A. W. Tozer writes: "The reason why many are still troubled, still seeking, still making little forward progress is because they have not yet come to the end of themselves. We are still giving some of the orders, and we are still interfering with God's working within us."

The interference we put up is our angst about advancing because we don't know what's next. Unlike the children, we want to know exactly what roads we will be driving down during this journey just in case one of them is too dangerous for us. We don't want any pain. We don't want any brokenness. We don't want any disappointment. We want smooth sailing — and we want to make sure that our hands are on the steering wheel helping the Lord drive.

But that's the beauty of this journey, the excitement that stirs us to go on. Knowing what's around the next corner has a way of lulling you to sleep during a trip. God, however, intends to keep us awake every step of the way, knowing that His direction for our lives is best because it brings about the refinement and purification that He so desires for each of us.

Christ's Heart in You

1. How has your journey molded and shaped you into the person you are?

2. How differently would your path have gone had you known ahead of time every outcome?

Pray: "Lord, show me what it means to trust You completely as I follow the course You have set for my life."?

<><

Day Three: His Assuring Promises

Once we begin traveling on this glorious journey with the Lord, we peer behind us. In the distance, we can still see the starting point. Bailing out would be easy since the road ahead is paved with unknown adventure and the road behind is clearly visible.

PursuingGod'sWord
Hebrews 6:13-20

We fidget and squirm. We contemplate how we ended up in this vehicle in the first place. "Isn't there an easier way to do this?" we ask ourselves. As our departure place becomes more desirable, what we need is some assurance — the touch of a calming hand that lets us know everything is going to be all right.

Our anxiety about pressing on with God is no surprise to Him. In His infinite wisdom, He knew that in order to keep us on this adventure with Him it would take more than a gesturing wave signaling us to follow Him. We need to know the assurance of His promises that this won't hurt and we will be all right.

The writer of Hebrews explains this to us. "God also bound Himself with an oath, so that those who received the promise could be perfectly sure that He would never change His mind. So God has given us both His promise and His oath. These two things are unchangeable because it is impossible for God to lie. Therefore, we who have fled to Him for refuge can take new courage, for we can hold on to His promise with confidence" (Hebrews 6:17-18, NLT).

With confidence, with assurance, we can go on. The writer concludes with one final point: "This confidence is like a strong and trustworthy anchor for our souls. It leads us through the curtain of heaven into God's inner sanctuary" (v. 19).

What is more assuring than an anchor? Faced with a stressful dilemma at an airport terminal, a young woman didn't know what to do. A lost ticket and a lost driver's license presented more problems than she could handle at the moment. And in that brief time she was left wondering if she would make it home that night as planned. She didn't need directions on how to get to her intended destination — she needed assurance that she would indeed get there.

He desires to see us through to our intended finishing point.

Jesus is our anchor. He's not going anywhere, and He desires to see us through to our intended finishing point. But He isn't always going to solve all of our problems instantaneously. What He will do is give us the peace we so desperately need in those moments of uncertainty along the way. Jesus told His disciples, "I am the way, the truth, and the life. No one can come to the Father except through me" (John 14:6).

When we understand that Jesus isn't going anywhere — He is with us for the long haul — then we can begin to traverse God's journey with unending hope and assurance.

Christ's Heart in You

1. How do God's promises in His Word assuage your fears?

2. What promises have meant the most to you on your journey with Christ?

Pray: "Lord, let Your deep assurances quiet my soul and, with Your peace, soothe any uneasiness I have."

<><

Day Four: Maintaining the Course

Momentary lapses in our determination are enough to send us skidding off course. God knows this journey of following Him and becoming the person He has created us to become isn't easy. But

Pursuing God's Word
1 Corinthians 10:1-13

through His grace and strength, it is possible to stay on track until we reach the final destination.

Noah was weak and worn out. Continually hammering pegs into his monstrous creation called an ark was enough to make any 500-year-old man ache with pain. He sat down beneath a tree in the shade for a moment to contemplate his disposition.

God will help us stand up to each trial as we continue on the journey He has set before us.

Noah could've easily quit, thrown down his hammer, and told God that enough was enough and if He really loved him, He would just speak a gigantic boat into existence. But Noah didn't.

The prospect of getting swept away in a worldwide flood was more than enough to encourage Noah to return to his duties. But the prospect that his actions would be deemed disobedient and irreverent was the deciding factor. Noah wanted to follow God no matter what — even if it meant looking like the biggest idiot on the planet by building a boat without any nearby water on which to sail.

Noah was still tired and worn out, so he probably muttered a quick prayer: "God, help me finish this project. I'm not capable of doing this on my own strength. I need You to give me the strength to endure."

The impending dip in the road sometimes seems too much to bear. This isn't just a short bump that we drive over and continue on. It's an event that could send us whipping around and returning to our starting point, which we mistakenly believe has comfort and certainty.

Francois Fenelon wrote about the grace God gives us to endure such trials and hardships: "We cannot see the extent of our future trials, nor of the vast supplies of which God is storing up in us so that we can meet them. And because we cannot see those future trials, nor the grace that will be needed for them, we are tempted to become discouraged and despondent in our present situations."

In encouraging the church in Corinth, Paul wrote: "Remember that the temptations that come into your life are no different from what others experience. And God is faithful. He will keep the temptation from becoming so strong that you can't stand up against it. When you are tempted, He will show you a way out so that you will not give in to it" (1 Corinthians 10:13).

The temptations — or trials — that we face in life are survivable. God will help us stand up to each trial as we continue on the journey He has set before us.

Fenelon writes that we can indeed endure when we understand God's omnipotent hand in this trek to follow Him: "We see our trials rolling in toward us like great, overpowering ocean waves. Our hearts fail us with fear at the prospect of drowning. We do not see that we stand within the point at which God, with a steady finger, has drawn the boundary line. Beyond that line the waves cannot pass."

Christ's Heart in You

1. What keeps your life's compass pointing toward God?

2. How do you handle moments of weakness in the journey?

Pray: "Lord, give me the strength I need to stay the course You have set before me."

<><

Day Five: The Final Destination

Knowing where we are going is paramount to our reaching the final destination. When we decide to follow God, we must understand what all this journey entails. We must also understand what awaits us in the end.

PursuingGod'sWord
John 6:60-71

In every good Indiana Jones action movie, we find our hero striking off on some journey through the jungle, or desert, or countryside. But he's not just out there in search of adventure — Dr. Jones is searching for a treasure. However, adventure just seems to find him.

The treasure that awaits us at the end of our journey is a deeper relationship with God. All the intimacy and excitement, love and adventure that we so desire in our relationships is found as we begin to seek God. When this relationship with God begins to grow as we follow Him wherever He leads, we desire for it to last forever. We desire deeply a life of eternity with Him, the lover of our soul.

Even in the beginning stages of their relationship with Jesus, the disciples understood that there was something vastly different about this man. The disciples sensed something great awaited them as they followed the Son of God. And as they began to sense this, they, too, desired to see this relationship last.

At one point in Jesus' ministry when many disciples began abandoning Him, Jesus looked at Peter and asked if he was going to leave as well. Peter simply answered, "Lord, to whom would we go? You alone have the words that give eternal life. We believe them, and we know that you are the Holy One of God" (John 6:68).

> *The treasure that awaits us at the end of our journey is an even deeper relationship with God.*

Peter had nowhere to go, but it didn't matter because he didn't desire to go anywhere. He wanted to be with the Son of God, the One whose words gave eternal life.

Eternal life boggles our minds when we dwell on it. Living forever? It seems like a faint dream. But the fact that it will actually come to pass and will be spent with our heavenly Father helps us understand that this journey is about getting to know the greatest lover of all time — the One who moved heaven and earth just to call us His own.

In the book *The Sacred Romance*, co-author John Eldredge explains what we will find when we reach our final destination: "For now, our life is a journey of high stakes and frequent danger. But we have turned the corner, the long years in exile are winding down and we are approaching home. There is no longer any question as to whether we will make it and if it will be good when we get there. ... One day soon we will round a bend in the road and our dreams will come true. We really will live happily ever after. The long years in exile will be swept away in the joyful tears of our arrival home. ... All we long for, we shall have; all we long to be, we will be."

Christ's Heart in You

1. What areas of your relationship with God do you want to see deepened?

2. How is your relationship with God related to your growth as a Christian?

Pray: "Lord, fill my heart with passion for relationship with You and give me the strength to stay committed to You."

<><

Your Pursuit

Compassionate Christianity

It is the duty of every Christian to be Christ to his neighbor.
— Martin Luther

Day One: Unfailing Devotion

To place our fingers on the pulse of God's heart is to find His compassion. It is more than just feeling empathetic toward the broken, the lost, the hurting. To shake our heads in sorrow at the brokenness surrounding us is nothing more than just recognizing the obvious. True compassion takes action.

PursuingGod'sWord
John 4:1-26

In our desire to see the attributes of God that we, too, want for our own lives, we must understand that He does not compartmentalize His nature. It is all encompassing. What's true of God in one area of His character is true in another. God, the unfailing One ever devoted to His children, is unfailing in His compassion for us.

Never does He display a certain attribute of His nature for a brief period of time. If it's for once, it's for always. And we, too, should ask the Lord to establish those same principles in our own hearts.

David understood compassion, although he didn't experience it from his earthly authority figures very often. King Saul felt little remorse for his relentless pursuit of David, but David's heart refused to grow embittered toward his king. And when it came to keeping his word, David was as faithful to honor it as was his heavenly Father.

Before his death, Jonathan asked David to take care of his family.

Among the survivors was Mephibosheth. A frail and weak child who was lame, Mephibosheth enjoyed the fruits of a compassionate heart in David. He dined with royalty. "As for Mephibosheth,' said the king, 'he shall eat at my table like one of the king's sons'" (2 Samuel 9:11).

No kingdom was ever advanced on intention alone.

David, seeing a boy in need of a father figure and a home, had compassion on Mephibosheth, partly because the boy was in need and partly because he wanted to honor his word to Jonathan. Regardless of the main thrust for his decision to show compassion, David did it, forever changing the course of a young boy's life.

If our compassion is not powered by hands and feet, our sympathy is like intending to cook a gourmet meal only to get no farther than pulling the pots from the cupboard. No kingdom was ever advanced on intention alone.

And David showed us that being devoted to intentions of compassion from long ago mimics the heart of God. Our devotion to God, our desire to be His hands and feet on earth, is shown when we act with compassion both today and in the future.

Oswald Chambers writes, "A person who has forgotten what God treasures will not be filled with joy. It is wonderful to remember that Jesus Christ has needs which we can meet — 'Give Me a drink' (John 4:7). How much kindness have I shown Him in the past week? Has my life been a good reflection upon His reputation?"

Let us not forget to be devoted to demonstrating compassion to a world in desperate need of it.

Christ's Heart in You

1. In what ways can you show more compassion to the people around you?

2. How have people shown you compassion in the past?

Pray: "Lord, fill me with a heart of compassion for people today."

<><

Day Two: Extending Grace

To understand the grace which God extends to all mankind is one of the first steps to understanding His heart of compassion. The next is to learn how to live a life of outstretched hands, extending that same grace to those around us.

PursuingGod'sWord
Joshua 6:12-27

Judging harshly those who have yet to have their eyes and hearts opened to the love of Christ shows how devoid of compassion Christians can be at times. Do our hearts break for the world around us, unknowingly lost in their sinful way of life? Do we see what God sees in them, the potential He has created them for in His Kingdom?

With Joshua leading the people of Israel into the Promised Land, the task of conquering the wicked nations seemed very devoid of compassion at times. But as we take a closer look, we see some of the best portraits of compassion in the Bible.

Sent to spy on Jericho, a couple of Israelites found refuge in the house of Rahab. She had heard of the amazing power their God possessed. She had heard the tales of deliverance, though they were 40 years old at this time. However, she knew there was something to them, and she didn't want to get caught in the fray.

We walk in grace as a result of the compassionate heart of God.

Rahab begged the Israelite spies to spare her life when they attacked Jericho. And instead of judging this woman for both her citizenship of this evil town and her harlotry, the spies extended a hand of grace. For at least a brief moment, they caught a glimpse of what she could become — better yet, of what God could do for and in her as well.

When the moment of truth came, we saw that God was faithful to this small, yet meaningful, extension of grace.

"And Joshua spared Rahab the harlot, her father's household, and all that she had. So she dwells in Israel to this day, because she hid the messengers whom Joshua sent to spy out Jericho" (Joshua 6:25).

Instead of being quick to judge, the compassion that touched Rahab's life changed her forever.

Steve Fry writes, "The truth is that we Christians sometimes treat unbelievers as enemies — it's 'them' against 'us.' This, of course, is a far cry from what the apostle Paul emphatically states in the fifth chapter of Romans, that, through Christ, all humankind has been reconciled to God, giving each of us the opportunity to receive God's gift of salvation. To put that another way, God's favor and forgiveness have been extended to all people everywhere because of what Jesus did on the cross. That is, indeed, good news."

We walk in grace as a result of the compassionate heart of God. As ambassadors of His name, we must be diligent to show that same grace to the world around us.

Christ's Heart in You

1. In what ways, both big and small, have you experienced God's grace in your life?

2. How can you extend grace to those you interact with on a daily basis?

Pray: "Lord, help me show grace to others just like You have shown me grace."

<><

Day Three: Broken for a People

We hear the stories of the inhumanity occurring halfway around the world. We see the pictures as well, and it stirs our hearts. More than likely, it evokes only a moment of emotion or a slow shake of the head and a glance down.

Pursuing**God's**Word
Nehemiah 2:1-9

But being moved emotionally for a group of needy people — even if it's just for a moment — is far from a heart of true compassion. If we have never seen the atrocities first-hand or cannot share in similarly painful experiences, it's hard to have anything more than distant empathy.

When the news that Jerusalem had been razed by dreadful enemies, Nehemiah's heart broke. And the action he took next demonstrated that what he felt was more than just momentary emotion — it was true compassion.

"So it was, when I heard these words, that I sat down and wept, and mourned for many days; I was fasting and praying before the God of heaven" (Nehemiah 1:4).

Nehemiah began fasting and praying. It was his people; he could relate to their experience. Instead of glibly shrugging his shoulders and going back to his comfortable lifestyle in the king's court, Nehemiah sought God's face on the matter. Was there anything for him to do? Did God want him to do anything? Was there any way he could make a difference miles from Jerusalem?

Although the situation may have made Nehemiah's heart sick, he waited upon God to open the right doors at the right time. At the right moment, Nehemiah struck, enabling him to receive the blessing of his king as well as empowering him to put hands and feet to the compassion welling up within him.

When God begins to stir our hearts, giving us compassion for a person or group of people, this is our signal to begin praying.

"Therefore the king said to me, 'Why is your face sad, since you are not sick? This is nothing but sorrow of heart.' So I became dreadfully afraid, and said to the king, 'May the king live forever! Why should my face not be sad, when the city, the place of my fathers' tombs, lies waste, and its gates are burned with fire?' Then the king said to me, 'What do you request?' So I prayed to the God of heaven" (Nehemiah 2:2-4).

God provided everything Nehemiah needed to act upon his compassionate heart. And it was because Nehemiah's compassion was filled with prayer.

When God begins to stir our hearts, giving us compassion for a person or group of people, this is our signal to begin praying. Does He want us to take some sort of action? If so, what is it? How do we accomplish what He wants us to do?

As this process becomes ingrained in our hearts, no longer will we think of compassion as merely evoking an emotion — it will evoke a change, both in our hearts and the people for whom we are broken.

Christ's Heart in You

1. How have stories you've heard about the poor, sick, or defenseless evoked a change in you?

2. What action can you take when your heart is moved with compassion?

Pray: "Lord, let my heart become one of compassion where I take action to help those in need."

<><

Day Four: Responding to Needs

PursuingGod'sWord
Mark 8:1-10

The suffering in our world is vast and unbelievable at times. Even if we feel our situations are painful, we can rest assured that someone else miles away knows a suffering we would never want to experience. And thinking about the amount of such pain and suffering spanning the globe overwhelms us.

No matter how compassionate we might be, it is easy for us to see the enormous amount of needs in this world and throw our hands in the air in despair. It seems impossible to meet all those needs. We wonder how we can make a difference.

When God calls us to action, we must act, regardless of how overwhelming the situation may appear.

Jesus, in feeding the four thousand, demonstrated how meeting needs from a heart of compassion is completely possible, regardless of how the situation appears. God — not us — makes this kind of compassion in action possible; and that's the premise under which we must operate.

"Jesus called His disciples to Him and said to them, 'I have compassion on the multitude, because they have now continued with Me three days and have nothing to eat. And if I send them away hungry to their own houses, they will faint on the way; for some of them have come from afar.' Then His disciples answered Him, 'How can one satisfy these people with bread here in the wilderness?'" (Mark 8:1-4).

Surely the disciples wanted to see these people fed as well, but they could not see how it was possible. Their question demonstrated their inability to see beyond themselves at that point. They were still living life as if they were alone and God were some distant figurehead in the sky.

Though they may have thought no "one" could satisfy, they were not alone. With Jesus in their presence, they quickly learned that even though "one" could not satisfy the hungry mass's needs, One could.

"So they ate and were filled, and they took up seven large baskets of leftover fragments" (Mark 8:8).

The stark reality is that we are unable to meet the needs of the world. It is heart-wrenching and deeply discouraging at times; however, God is completely capable of meeting every need of every person in every country of the world. Though His life overflowed with compassion, Jesus did not attempt to meet every need with a world tour. Instead, He let His life and death embody compassion, teaching us to trust God to meet all those needs just as He did.

When God calls us to action, we must act, regardless of how overwhelming the situation may appear. And instead of bemoaning how we aren't making much of a difference, we need to ask Him to do it, to empower us to make a difference where He calls us to be and to trust that He will make a difference where we aren't.

Man's heart of compassion does not even compare to God's compassionate nature. However, when we learn to trust Him to meet the needs toward those we cannot reach, our heart of compassion grows as does our faith in Him.

Christ's Heart in You

1. How can you respond when you hear of such injustices worldwide?

2. How can you make a difference when God calls you to action?

Pray: "Lord, help me to trust in You to bring about a change in desperate situations and to participate however You ask."

Day Five: Freedom in Forgiveness

Before we discovered God's love for us, we walked around in shackles and chains to our sin. We felt condemned and hopeless, unable to loose the dangling albatross from around our necks. We felt no freedom.

> **PursuingGod'sWord**
> John 8:1-12

Yet freedom came like a crashing wave of God's love and grace, opening our eyes to His amazing plan of redemption for us and all of mankind. Suddenly, we were free to be who He created us to be.

Unfortunately, we sometimes forget that experience. And instead of offering the keys to unloosing the chains of the bound world, we offer to tighten their chains, spewing words of condemnation instead of words of hope and love.

It was the Pharisees grand plan: trap Jesus into contradicting the law with His new brand of religion and convince the masses He was a heretic. They had tried this ploy many times before with no success, but this time there was a gleam of hope in their eyes as they dragged the aduleress through the streets.

"They said to Him, 'Teacher, this woman was caught in adultery, in the very act. Now Moses, in the law, commanded us that such should be stoned. But what do you say?' This they said, testing Him, that they might have something of which to accuse Him. But Jesus stooped down and wrote on the ground with His finger, as though He did not hear. So when they continued asking Him, He raised Himself up and said to them, 'He who is without sin among you, let him throw a stone at her first'" (John 8:4-7).

Jesus displayed the heart of God with such fullness and beauty that it should drive us to do the same.

One by one the stones fell to the ground as the Pharisees slowly walked away, disappointed that Jesus once again foiled them with a wise answer. Then He quickly dismissed the woman, telling her, "Neither do I condemn you; go and sin no more" (v. 11).

Not only did Jesus release the adulteress, He released the Pharisees. He did not seek to heap condemnation on their heads either — He simply sought to prove that no one is without sin. And neither is anyone without the opportunity to receive forgiveness!

Though Jesus saw right through the Pharisees' deceitful ploys, He didn't lash out at them. He sought to show them the danger of a judgmental heart.

In one dramatic scene in the Bible, we see Jesus pouring out compassion long before He traveled to the hill of Calvary. Down in the city amidst a confused people, Jesus displayed the heart of God with such fullness and beauty that it should drive us to do the same.

Instead of condemning the world around us for their sinful nature, we should act as Jesus did, extending forgiveness to those who don't even know they need it. It may be the only way they ever see the heart of God.

Christ's Heart in You

1. How can you show Christ-like forgiveness to those around you?

2. Have you been holding someone captive by not forgiving that person? If so, release it to God and make things right with that person.

Pray: "Lord, give me Your heart of forgiveness so I may share the love of Christ with the world around me."

<><

<u>Your Pursuit</u>

Closer than a Brother

---

*A man is the sum of his parts and his character
the sum of the traits that compose it.*
— A.W. Tozer

Day One: Never Jealous

Jonathan had every reason in the world to be
jealous. As the heir to the throne of his father
King Saul, Jonathan had just watched some
young man slay Israel's biggest foe with one twirl of his slingshot. This
man, David, returned to Jerusalem as the nation's hero. Suddenly, all the
attention Jonathan had received was now being turned in the direction of
David. Jonathan was probably irritated — but then he heard David speak.

| PursuingGod'sWord |
| 1 Samuel 18:1-4 |

David told King Saul who he was, explaining where his strength
came from. It wasn't from the accuracy of his slingshot; rather, it came
from the Lord. And that was all Jonathan needed to hear.

"Now when he had finished speaking to Saul, the soul of Jonathan
was knit to the soul of David, and Jonathan loved him as his own soul. …
Then Jonathan made a covenant with David because he loved him as his
own soul" (1 Samuel 18:1,3).

In our friendships with others, we must be careful to guard
against jealousy. So often, we see people doing great things in whatever
they set their hand to do, and we can develop a jealous spirit toward them.
Jealousy's most damaging consequence is that it prevents us from walking
in the unity of the Spirit to which we, as believers, are called to live. Paul
exhorts us to live at peace with all men. (Romans 12:18) But that is so difficult to do when we envy someone's current situation.

As heir to the throne, Jonathan had it all. He had power, wealth,
fame. He even had a claim to the throne of Israel. But when he heard

David speak, Jonathan's heart melted. Jonathan saw something different in the life of David — his faith, his confidence, his assurance. And Jonathan was drawn to him. "Why be envious of the anointing on this man?" Jonathan probably thought to himself.

True love for our brothers and sisters in Christ ... contains no jealousy.

When we accept the Lord as our Savior, we knit ourselves to the body of Christ. God is moving through and among His people in different ways. Just because one person is gifted in one area doesn't mean we should ever be jealous of what the Lord has given them. God imparts gifts in different measures to all His people. Jonathan was given an amazing ability to lead; however, he also had the capacity to support David, for they had a covenant that ran deep.

In 1 Corinthians 13, Paul expounds on what true love is. And not surprisingly, Paul included this line in verse 4: "Love is not jealous." True love for our brothers and sisters in Christ — in our friendships, in our relationships, in our families — contains no jealousy. God wants to use us all to accomplish His Kingdom plans. And He wants us to do it together, standing strong and firm with one another, united for the purpose of advancing His Kingdom.

Christ's Heart in You

1. How has jealousy affected any of your past relationships?

2. How can you be more supportive of those in leadership over you?

Pray: "Lord, I want to participate in Your plan for the body of Christ. Use me in whatever way You see fit."

<><

Day Two: A Protection

No longer was inheriting the throne a concern for Jonathan. He never felt threatened by this young upstart named David. All Jonathan knew was that the hand of the Lord was upon David, and Jonathan desired to see him reach the destiny that God had for him. For

PursuingGod'sWord
1 Samuel 19:1-7

when trouble arose, Jonathan was there to assist David.

As David's popularity began to grow, Saul began to fear what the people might do. He saw the possibility that David might dethrone him. So, instead of going on the defensive, Saul — ever the field general — decided to attack David first.

"Now Saul spoke to Jonathan his son and to all his servants, that they should kill David; but Jonathan, Saul's son, delighted greatly in David. So Jonathan told David, saying, 'My father Saul seeks to kill you. Therefore please be on your guard until morning, and stay in a secret place and hide. And I will go out and stand beside my father in the field where you are, and I will speak with my father about you. Then what I observe, I will tell you.'" (1 Samuel 19:1-3).

True friends are people who will stand as a shield for us. David and Jonathan's friendship would have never gone anywhere had Jonathan not been willing to risk his life by protecting David.

True love in our friendships is one that seeks to cover.

In our relationships with others, we need to be careful to guard their trust by protecting them in difficult situations instead of exposing them. If Jonathan really wanted to betray David, all he had to do was kill him. Jonathan had complete access to David, for David trusted him. Or if he felt too guilty about stabbing his friend in the back, Jonathan could inform his father of David's whereabouts. But Jonathan protected him.

In Genesis 9, we learn of a similar situation with Noah. After the ark came to rest, Noah got drunk and naked in his tent. Ham, instead of covering his father, exposed his father Noah's naked and drunken state. Shem and Japheth, however, covered their father.

We must ask ourselves what kind of people we want to be — Do we want to expose our friends? Or do we want to cover them?

True love in our friendships is one that seeks to cover. During Jesus' time on earth, He constantly spoke out against those people who sought to expose the sinners. When the Pharisees were dragging the woman caught in the act of adultery through the streets, the Pharisees were preparing to stone her before Jesus asked for the person without sin to throw the first stone. They all dropped their stones and left.

God is in the business of covering our sins. He hands us robes of righteousness to cover the ugliness that rests beneath. And we too should seek to be people who act in accordance with the heartbeat of our heavenly Father, seeking to cover and protect whenever the opportunity arises.

Christ's Heart in You

1. How well do you protect your friends?

2. How can you better "cover" those you are in relationship with?

Pray: "Lord, help me to be one who protects rather than exposes in my relationships."

<><

Day Three: A Servant

Sometimes in our relationships with others, we view the other person as someone from whom we constantly make withdrawals. We see our friends as people who can do things for us, get things for us, help us accomplish our goals. But that's not what Jonathan and David's friendship was about.

| PursuingGod'sWord |
| 1 Samuel 20:1-11 |

While in the king's palace, Jonathan was the one who was waited on hand and foot. However, in his friendship with David, Jonathan became a gracious servant.

"'And I will go out and stand beside my father in the field where you are, and I will speak with my father about you. Then what I observe, I will tell you.' Thus Jonathan spoke well of David to Saul his father, and said to him, 'Let not the king sin against his servant, against David, because he has not sinned against you, and because his works have been very good toward you.'" (1 Samuel 20:3-4).

What a friend Jonathan was to David! In the midst of one of the most challenging times in David's life, Jonathan issued words that would put any person's anxious heart at ease. The man with power to change things with the command of his voice said he would do whatever David asked him to do. This is the heart of a servant.

So often we forget what it's like to be a servant, what it's like to serve with a pure heart for the Lord. Being a servant doesn't mean we are doormats for our friends, overextending ourselves just because they ask us to do something. But when people are really in need of help, can we be counted on — even when it's not convenient?

Servants are those people who have given up their "right" to live a self-gratifying life. It's not a call to monasticism or pious solitude; rather, servanthood is a call to demonstrate the love of Christ to others through helping them reach what God has called them to do. Jonathan was a servant toward David.

Servants are those people who have given up their "right" to live a self-gratifying life.

People who are willing to serve the Lord in every capacity will find a special home in heaven. Not everyone is willing to abandon their lives for the Lord, serving the body of Christ. But holding onto our lives on earth — something that's so temporal it's only a blink in comparison to eternity — is worthless. The benefits of serving Christ, however, are priceless. In Mark 10:31, Jesus tells His disciples, "But many who are first will be last, and the last first."

Jesus never tries to manipulate us with His words. However, He does encourage us to do the thing that's most representative of the Father's love. God gives us everything we need to accomplish the goals that He sets before us in life — why not give it back to Him and others with a servant's heart?

Just like Jonathan said to David, God tells us the same thing: "Call to Me, and I will answer you, and show you great and mighty things, which you do not know" (Jeremiah 33:3).

Christ's Heart in You

1. How are you a servant to others?

2. How can you serve more in your relationships with other people?

Pray: "Lord, fill me with a servant's heart today."

Day Four: Selfless Love

With each passing moment, the popularity of David grew — and so did Saul's hatred for him. Jonathan's love for David, however, grew stronger. For whatever reason, he could see the anointing that rested upon David. All King Saul saw was his family dynasty on the throne starting and stopping with himself.

PursuingGod'sWord
1 Samuel 20:24-40

One night when David wasn't seated at the royal dinner table in the palace, Saul became angry, demanding Jonathan to reveal David's whereabouts.

"Then Saul's anger was aroused against Jonathan, and he said to him, 'You son of a perverse, rebellious woman! Do I not know that you have chosen the son of Jesse to your own shame and to the shame of your mother's nakedness? For as long as the son of Jesse lives on the earth, you shall not be established, nor your kingdom. Now therefore, send and bring him to me, for he shall surely die.' And Jonathan answered Saul his father, and said to him, 'Why should he be killed? What has he done?'" (1 Samuel 20:30-32).

We must be diligent to lay down our lives in every possible situation.

What was of utmost importance to Saul — establishing a legacy upon the throne and seeing Jonathan become king — was of no importance to Jonathan, especially if it meant that he had to betray his best friend. His friendship ran deeper than a seat upon the throne of Israel.

The selfless love that Jonathan demonstrated in his friendship with David is one we should all desire to have in our own relationships with people. Was it worth betraying the trust of David so he could maintain his rightful place upon the throne of Israel? Jonathan thought not.

We see this same type of sacrifice, this selfless love, modeled perfectly in the life of Jesus. Our Savior wasn't interested in satisfying His desires — He only wanted to lay down everything He had for the salvation of mankind and the glory of God. In Jesus' relationships with those around Him, He gave all of Himself. And He ultimately gave all of Himself to everyone, dying on the Cross to save us all from the punishment for our sins.

What would it have profited Jonathan to hold onto what he did have? Instead of being a model of what a true friend should be, he would have been a footnote to Saul's reign over Israel — some prince who died in battle. But what a legacy he left behind instead!

As people who seek to live a life pleasing to Christ, we must be diligent to lay down our lives in every possible situation. When we look around and see our friends in desperate need of our help, it's not time to be thinking about ourselves. Are we going to be a people who help those around us arrive at the destination the Lord has intended for them, allowing our lives to be used for His purposes?

Christ's Heart in You

1. How can you help those around you reach the purpose God has for their lives?

2. What sacrifices can you make for friends in your life?

Pray: "Lord, show me what it means to live a life of sacrifice in my relationships with You and others."

<><

Day Five: Unending Loyalty

Many times, our kindness toward others — including our friends — is dictated by convenience or some underlying motive. However, true kindness and love toward others isn't concerned about what it gets in return. We always reap what we sow.

PursuingGod'sWord
2 Samuel 9:1-7

Jonathan had sown unending loyalty in his friendship with David. Despite King Saul's concern that David would take Jonathan's rightful place upon the throne, Jonathan continued to remain loyal to David. In every situation, Jonathan was faithful to keep harm from coming upon him. And after Jonathan died, his friendship paid wonderful dividends for his son, Mephibosheth.

"Now David said, 'Is there still anyone who is left of the house of Saul, that I may show him kindness for Jonathan's sake?' ... Now when Mephibosheth, the son of Jonathan, the son of Saul, had come to David, he fell on his face and prostrated himself. Then David said, 'Mephibosheth?' And he answered, 'Here is your servant!' So David said to him, 'Do not fear for I will surely show you kindness for Jonathan your father's sake, and will restore to you all the land of Saul your grandfather; and you shall eat bread at my table continually'" (2 Samuel 9:1, 6-7).

A.W. Tozer writes, "A man is the sum of his parts and his character the sum of the traits that compose it."

David's character was one of loyalty toward Jonathan. David's love toward Jonathan was genuine and true. This ruddy shepherd boy from the hills of Israel wasn't friends with Jonathan simply to avoid Saul's unjust wrath — David's heart was knit to Jonathan's heart. Their friendship was a lasting one, a friendship that transcended time, continuing long after Jonathan was dead.

In our friendships, we must be careful to maintain pure motives.

In our friendships, we must be careful to maintain pure motives. When we are friends with others for the wrong reasons, our fraudulent behavior will be exposed. A test or trial is coming when we're going to need to rely upon the body of believers around us. The Lord is Who our trust should be founded upon, but others holding us up encourage and strengthen us.

There came a day when Jonathan needed someone to look after his son, Mephibosheth. Jonathan was dead, so who would do such a thing? Only a loyal friend such as David. Mephibosheth didn't just avoid the normal fate that befell heirs of past dethroned kings — he feasted at the table of David.

"As for Mephibosheth," said [King David], "he shall eat at my table like one of the king's sons" (2 Samuel 9:11).

Let us prove our friendships to be true and genuine, our love for those around us to be real with no hidden agendas. Jesus demonstrated the same type of love toward us — why shouldn't we do the same?

Christ's Heart in You

1. What motivates you to be faithful in your friendships?

2. How can you remain loyal to your friends through difficult times?

Pray: "Lord, purify my motives in my friendships and help me to be a loyal friend."

<>＜

Your Pursuit

Ablaze on the Altar

I know Him, because He first knew me, and continues to know me. He knows me as a friend, One who loves me; and there is no moment when His eye is off me, or His attention distracted from me, and no moment, therefore, when His care falters.

— J.I. Packer

Day One: Our Sin

Once we come to know Christ in an intimate and personal relationship, we begin to understand that the call is deep. For

> Pursuing**God'sWord**
> Hebrews 9:23-28

some, the call is too deep as they shy away from what looks like the stripping away of all their freedom. For others, the result of the call is attractive, but the sacrifice required to reach the fullness of what God has is too much. And still for another group, the call is consuming, beginning with a series of sacrifices that places them in close communion with God.

Half-hearted commitments are no commitments at all. And if we ever expect to experience the fullness of what our heavenly Father has for us, we must be willing to be consumed, to place on the altar those things which prevent us from enjoying everything God has intended for our lives.

Placing our sin on the altar is the place to begin. For most of us, it was recognition of our sin that drove us to God in the first place, realizing how much is in our lives and how much we truly detest it. Yet, it's so attractive in its own twisted way. We know that it is a cold, detestable lump of coal, but when we glance its way, it morphs into a seductive object of beauty. Despite our best efforts to resist it, we realize we will never be able to conquer it until we place it upon the altar and let it burn.

Our reluctance to do so weighs heavily upon us, but not until we allow the truth to take root in our hearts does our reluctance stop haunting us. Sin must die a violent death — and Jesus has already done so in order for us to have freedom from its alluring ways.

"And as it is appointed for men to die once, but after this the judgment, so Christ was offered once to bear the sins of many. To those who eagerly wait for Him He will appear a second time, apart from sin, for salvation" (Hebrews 9:27-28).

> *We must place recurring sin in our lives on the altar and leave it there.*

Every time we choose to yield to sin, we torture ourselves by embracing lies. But Jesus was crucified once and for all, covering the eternal consequences of our sin. With that knowledge, we must place the recurring sin in our lives on the altar and leave it there. Instead of gingerly holding sin's hand while squeezing the Savior's, we must release the sin in our life by torching it.

With each decision we make in our lives to choose life, to choose God's way, we burn sin. We heap more flames on its charred head until its beauty fades to ashes. It is the heart of God for us to choose Him. And He is pleased by our doing so.

Let us be faithful in the call He has placed upon our lives, determining to let Jesus' sacrifice stand for our sin once and for all, choosing God's way over sin's in each and every situation.

Christ's Heart in You

1. What areas of your life do you struggle to place on the altar?

2. If there are some areas of sin you need to put to death in your heart, pray about it and find a friend to hold you accountable to your decision.

Pray: "Lord, help me walk in freedom from sin as I relinquish the things I've held onto."

<><

Day Two: Our Plans

It was a day Simon Peter would never forget, a day that started like most others that ended in the beginning of one extraordinary adventure with a man named Jesus. Peter knew the right moment to toss his nets into the constant tide — he just didn't know that this day the tide would bring

> **PursuingGod'sWord**
> Matthew 4:18-22

him more than he ever imagined.

"And Jesus, walking by the Sea of Galilee, saw two brothers, Simon, called Peter, and Andrew, his brother, casting a net into the sea; for they were fisherman. Then He said to them, 'Follow Me, and I will make you fishers of men.' They immediately left their nets and followed Him" (Matthew 4:18-20).

The future for Peter was as predictable as the ebb and flow of the tide. He knew all the particulars by this point in his life after watching his elders model life as a fisherman. The predictability of it all made life as fishermen quite comfortable for Peter, even if the fishing wasn't precitably prosperous. However, there was something in Peter, an urge to leave his nets and go after something much more alluring.

He is longing for us to place our plans on the altar and pursue His with all that we are.

After years of following Jesus, both before and after His death, Peter wrote, "Therefore humble yourselves under the mighty hand of God, that He may exalt you in due time, casting all your care upon Him, for He cares for you" (1 Peter 5:6-7).

The voice of experience bodes promise for us. These words come from a man who wasn't afraid to leave his livelihood behind without a thought to where his provision would come from. This was a man who wasn't afraid to leap out of a boat and charge across a raging sea just to be with Jesus. This was a man who saw that comfort and predictability paled in comparison to life on the edge with Christ.

So, with the release of his nets that crashed to the shore's edge, Peter set ablaze that lifestyle that appeared so attractive to him for so long. Though he knew the future was completely unknown, he felt more confident setting it on fire and venturing out into a plan that belonged to someone else than remaining trapped in its comfortable grip — a grip that had slowly begun to squeeze true life right out of him.

God has adventuresome plans for us all, but far too many times we elect to decline that option for the comfort of our own. While a life on the edge with the Lord seems attractive, the risk appears too great. We wonder, "What if it doesn't work out like it did for Peter? What if I don't like it? What if it's foolish?"

Yet, with risk comes great reward. No company ever made its first million by investing in a neighborhood lemonade stand — a venture that could make a few dollars on a torrid day but would never bankrupt the investors.

That voice we hear whispering — at other times, screaming — is the Lord, yearning for us to explore a life with Him. He is longing for us to place our plans on the altar and pursue His with all that we are. While we wonder if we can afford to do it, the question God wants to know is this: Can our burning hearts afford not to?

Christ's Heart in You

1. What fears keep you from pursuing the fullness of God's plan for your life?

2. Do you feel as though You are grasping all God has for you or are you missing something? Why?

Pray: "Lord, show me the fullness of Your plan for my life and give me the courage to pursue it."

<><

Day Three: Our Comfort

Once people make the brave step of faith in receiving Christ as Lord and Savior, they sometimes mistakenly believe that entrance to the kingdom of heaven is enough. They assume that admission to God's celestial home is what the goal is. After all, it's why we chose to follow Him, right?

Pursuing God's Word
2 Corinthians 12:7-11

Many believers act as if that's the only reason they made a profession of faith. They don't want to spend eternity in hell, so they opt for the most desirable option. Occasionally, they will do something for the church just to remind themselves what a loving God they serve, but they quickly return to the comfort with which they have surrounded themselves.

However, Christianity has nothing to do with comfort as we have so delicately crafted it for ourselves. God does not want us to suffer, but the notion that comfortable living is what following Him is all about is an idea that needs readjusting.

To live in constant comfort is to live constantly within the bubble of inactivity — we aren't storming into the enemy's territory and reclaiming what he has unjustly taken; therefore, we pose no real threat to him. To be left alone by the enemy also means we are left alone in our quiet, debilitating thought. So mired in our comfort are we that we never walk outside into the turmoil surrounding us to see what might become of a few encounters with seeking souls.

No one demonstrates the power of shirking comfort for the Lord better than the apostle Paul. It wasn't that Paul sought out pain and suffering in order to make himself look more holy and righteous, but when those afflictions found him, he didn't run — he embraced them for what they were and continued forging ahead into the calling God had placed on his life.

To be left alone by the enemy also means we are left alone in our quiet, debilitating thought.

Paul writes, "And He said to me, 'My grace is sufficient for you, for My strength is made perfect in weakness.' Therefore most gladly I will rather boast in my infirmities, that the power of Christ may rest upon me. Therefore I take pleasure in infirmities, in reproaches, in needs, in persecutions, in distresses, for Christ's sake. For when I am weak, then I am strong" (2 Corinthians 12:9-10).

Following God doesn't mean that smooth sailing rests ahead. He does prepare the way for us, but that doesn't imply an uneventful journey with nothing but blessings and happiness. God wants His best for His children, but His best for us came at a large price, a tag that included an excruciating experience both for the Son and the Father. However, it is during that time that God's finest work came to completion.

And so it is with us. If we are willing to sacrifice our comfort at times, setting it ablaze for the kingdom of God, we will eventually be able to enjoy the incredible fruit that comes from a toiling labor.

Christ's Heart in You

1. How often do you venture beyond your comfort zone? Why?

2. What are some areas of comfort you can sacrifice for Christ?

Pray: "Lord, help me to resist the urge to live a life of comfort, instead exchanging my life for a life of true sacrifice."

<><

Day Four: Our Fears

In desiring to see God consume us completely, we are oftentimes held back by the fear of the unknown. The first step is the hardest as our

PursuingGod'sWord
Judges 6:21-27

feet remain firmly planted in the comfortable place where we are. We have no idea what lies ahead — and at least from where we currently stand, we have a good idea of what will happen if we don't move.

Not many images of bravery in the Bible stirs our hearts like the one of Gideon with just 300 men holding torches and pitchers, standing on a cliff overlooking a valley of thousands of enemy soldiers. His confidence that God would lead the Israelites into victory was enormous. In fact, Gideon knew he couldn't lose — it was impossible.

If we want God to do great things with our lives, we must place our fears upon His altar and watch them disappear in smoke.

That image is a far cry from our first picture of Gideon, who cowered in a winepress for fear of being killed by the Midianites. Yet as he yielded to God, apprehensively taking the first step, Gideon's fear was set ablaze. And for Gideon, he began to set fear ablaze on the altar by tearing one down.

Though the angel of the Lord called Gideon a "mighty man of valor," it was the potential of what God saw in him and even created him to be, not what he was at the moment. At the moment, he was a quaking, anxious young man, unsure about how to conquer his fears, much less how to carry out the frightening task assigned him. "You shall save Israel from the hand of the Midianites. Have I not sent you?" (Judges 6:14).

And it all began with Gideon tearing down his father's altars to Baal. "The Lord said to [Gideon], 'Take your father's young bull, the second bull of seven years old, and tear down the altar of Baal that your father has, and cut down the wooden image that is beside it; and build an altar to the Lord your God on top of this rock in the proper arrangement, and take the second bull and offer a burnt sacrifice with the wood of the image which you shall cut down.' So Gideon took ten men from among his servants and did as the Lord had said to him. But because he feared his father's household and the men of the city too much to do it by day, he did it by night" (v. 25-27).

Before Gideon saved a nation, he began by facing his fears — albeit in a reluctant way at night — and obeyed God. In the night, Gideon set ablaze the fear that haunted him, allowing him to gain confidence that the Lord would sustain him no matter how difficult the task or situation.

If we want God to do great things with our lives, we must place our fears upon His altar and watch them disappear in smoke. For when we go with God, the fear that we will fail disappears in light of His love and perfect guidance and direction.

Christ's Heart in You

1. How has fear held you back from pursuing God's heart for you?

2. What fears can you lay on the altar for Christ so you can pursue God more deeply?

Pray: "Lord, give me the courage to overcome areas in my life that have hindered me from pursuing You."

<><

Day Five: Our Lives

When the Holy Spirit moves upon our hearts to take immediate action, we know it. Our pulse elevates, our mouth dries out — and our confidence in God swells, cascading over the fear that we might be acting on emotion and impulse. And while it felt good to obey, we quietly wonder what it might take for us to live a life that daily experiences such heart-racing excitement. We wonder if it's possible to live a life that encompasses what it means to live for Him, that at almost every moment of decision in life we see His guiding hand — and we follow it.

> Pursuing God's Word
> Acts 7:1-60

Such a life is the culmination of seeing our sin, our plans, our comfort, and our fears placed shamelessly upon the altar of our lives, placing all that we are right there with them. As they disappear beneath God's burning flame, we begin to realize for the first time what being a Christian is all about.

No longer do we yearn for another exciting program in our churches or another emotionally driven conference. No longer do we look forward to another sermon that stirs our hearts, even though it has been six months since we heard one last. No longer are we trying to look like we are sacrificing our lives when we've stacked the altar with wet wood.

What we are longing for is the next moment we hear God's voice in our lives and can respond immediately in obedience. We are longing for our next chance — no matter where it may be — to see God directly interact in our lives and the lives of those around us. We are longing for the next chance to prove our faithfulness, embracing it with boldness and confidence that God will prove His faithfulness yet again to us.

> *We are longing for the next chance to prove our faithfulness.*

In studying the life of Stephen, we hear in his words and see in his actions that he lived life this way. He had long since placed his life upon the altar before his life culminated with a confrontation with angry religious leaders. So, the choice of what to do when the situation arose was no choice at all: Stephen's choice to advance the kingdom of God was predetermined by him.

When his teachings were called into question, Stephen delivered a fiery, passionate message that stirs us still today. It's a call to respond to Christ.

Stephen knew the consequences of his actions might be dire, even fatal, but moments like these were what his life was all about. If even one person decided to follow Christ from what he said, it would be worth it. Undoubtedly, Stephen was at peace as his stoning commenced.

Though lifting the carcass of our flesh upon the altar and burning it may be difficult to do all at once, we can lighten the burden piece by piece. And as we do, our faith in God grows — and our entire lives will be consumed in a flame of love for the One we worship.

Christ's Heart in You

1. What areas of your life have you already sacrificed to God?

2. What areas of your life can you sacrifice to God now?

Pray: "Lord, make my life a constant sacrifice to You in all that I do."

<><

Your Pursuit

Advancing the Kingdom

How do you convince a world that God is alive? By His aliveness in your life, by His work in producing reality in your experience.
— Howard G. Hendricks

Day One: Through Grace

Advancing the kingdom of God is unlike advancing any earthly kingdom. The might and force used to overtake the old kingdom and replace it with God's takes place on our knees in prayer. But the "combat" of day-to-day living is won with a much more gentle approach.

> **PursuingGod'sWord**
> Romans 12

In demonstrating the power of God's kingdom to others, we must take on the attributes of Christ. One such characteristic is grace. Never did Jesus bludgeon others over the head with God's Word and scream condemnation upon them. Who would want to serve a King whose primary agenda was manipulating His servants into submission through guilt and scare tactics?

As the scribes and Pharisees dragged the adulterous woman through the streets and berated her for her sins in front of Jesus, we see an example of what Jesus knew to be an effective way to advance the Gospel. Though the Pharisees' motive was simply to trap Jesus with the law, they gave Jesus a golden opportunity to show everyone within earshot and beyond what God's kingdom was all about.

"So when they continued asking [Jesus], He raised Himself up and said to them, 'He who is without sin among you, let him throw a stone at her first.' And again He stooped down and wrote on the ground. Then those who heard it, being convicted by their conscience, went out one by one, beginning with the oldest even to the last. And Jesus was left alone, and the woman standing in the midst. . . . Jesus said to her, 'Neither do I condemn you; go and sin no more'" (John 8:7-9, 11).

God's kingdom is founded on grace.

Grace is the most illogical action. It goes against what we perceive as truth and justice. Why would someone just wipe the slate clean for no reason at all? There has to be a hidden agenda, right? Do we have the capacity to shower grace on someone when we know what he truly deserves?

But God's kingdom is founded on grace. It's what allows us to become children of the living God. It's what washes us clean from our sins. It's what saves us from the fate we also deserve.

As we understand the principles upon which God's kingdom is founded, we are enabled to advance His kingdom with greater ease and understanding. Applying the principles of God's kingdom into our lifestyles, we begin to embody Christ to others. We put flesh on the Word of God — and others cannot look away. The beauty of Christ is enrapturing, capturing the eyes of those around us as He shines through us.

In determining to demonstrate God's grace as He has shown it to us, we will present His kingdom to a destitute world in a way they have never seen it. And not only will it capture their eyes — it will capture their hearts.

Christ's Heart in You

1. How has a demonstration of grace impacted your life?

2. How has your understanding of grace transformed your view of God?

Pray: "Lord, fill my life with grace as I show others the same grace You have shown me."

<><

Day Two: Through Love

Although Jesus' message of salvation was most effective with a race of people waiting expectantly for a Savior, He never hesitated to spread the Gospel message around to Gentiles. It was who He was

Pursuing God's Word
Acts 7:1-60

— the Word of God made flesh so that the world may see the Father's love. Our actions, too, put flesh on what we profess with our mouths. To say that God is our loving King whom we serve, only to live way outside His commandments, demonstrates that our hearts are elsewhere. A true heart of love advances God's kingdom—hypocrisy sends it into retreat.

When Jesus asked the Samaritan woman for a drink, His mere words of conversation spoke volumes about His Father's love. She was a Samaritan — Jews and Samaritans didn't speak. But Jesus sought to share the Gospel with her, to show her the way, regardless of what nationality she was.

> *Love ... points the way to God's heart.*

Love does not condemn; rather, it points the way to God's heart, capturing the essence of what His kingdom is all about. And we see how Jesus pierced the heart of the Samaritan woman without condemning her, revealing a heart of love that drew her to Him.

Jesus said, "You worship what you do not know; we know what we worship, for salvation is for the Jews. But the hour is coming, and now is, when the true worshipers will worship the Father in spirit and truth; for the Father is seeking such to worship Him" (John 4:22-23).

Love was already being communicated to this woman, but for her to realize that she, too, could join in this wonderful plan of salvation, worshiping God just as anyone else could, filled her with life. Instead of living as an outcast, she could share in the joy of worshiping God, just like all the Jews. No longer was she left in the distance — she could experience His presence in her life as close as her skin. She was understanding this love. With this newfound knowledge, she could not control herself. Her life had been touched and she would never be the same.

That's what God's love has done for us: it has transformed us — an on-going evolution — into more and more of what God desires for us to be. And in the process, His kingdom is advanced. The fruit of God's love in our lives cannot be denied by anyone, and people are drawn to its beauty. The love of God penetrates our deepest wounds and refreshes our souls, leaving us to see the bright future He has always envisioned for our lives.

Christ's Heart in You

1. How has God's love impacted the way you think about Him?

2. How can you show the love of Christ to others in a practical way today?

Pray: "Lord, help me to share Your love with others today."

<><

Day Three: Through Truth

There are times in life when we are so absorbed in a line of thought that we cannot see beyond it. The foundation of our thought process is fashioned in such a way that to think in another manner would be impossible. What we know as truth guides our reasoning.

PursuingGod'sWord
John 3:9-21

In advancing the kingdom of God, it is so important for us to teach the truth of the Gospel to others. There are people who have been held in so much bondage that they have begun to accept the lies of the enemy as truth — and it thwarts their decision-making capabilities. It should be no wonder people living in darkness choose sin as a way of life; they believe that is the truth.

Groomed to be a Pharisee, Nicodemus had a difficult time receiving the truth from Jesus, yet it intrigued him. The message Jesus preached sounded good, but was it real? The question loomed large in the mind of Nicodemus, who was hungry for an answer. He couldn't understand what Jesus meant by a second birth, so he asked Jesus to explain Himself.

The truth sets us free because we no longer have to live in the shadow of lies.

"Nicodemus answered and said to Him, 'How can these things be?' Jesus answered and said to him, 'Are you the teacher of Israel, and do not know these things? Most assuredly, I say to you, We speak what We know and testify what We have seen, and you do not receive Our witness. . . . he who does the truth comes to the light, that his deeds may be clearly seen, that they have been done in God'" (John 3:9-11, 21).

Nicodemus struggled to see how Jesus could be telling the truth because a second birth seemed impossible. What was He talking about?

But when Jesus explained the truth, Nicodemus understood. The truth is that our lives are made new in Christ. His birth, life, death, and resurrection show us step-by-step God's plan to win the hearts of people across the face of the earth. And in understanding the truth behind God's love for us, the kingdom of God is advanced.

The truth sets us free because we no longer have to live in the shadow of lies. No longer do we have to believe the enemy's tricks. Instead, we begin to spot these tactics nearly immediately, tearing them down with the help of the Lord as we call on Him.

As God reveals His truth to us, we cannot resist Him for very long without defiantly rebelling against His leading in our lives. When we start to walk in the light of the truth that God has laid out for all His children, we will experience the fullness of what His kingdom can do — and those hidden in darkness will be drawn toward the light, living testaments of an advancing kingdom.

Christ's Heart in You

1. What truths have you learned that have transformed the way you view God?

2. How have truths freed you from things that held you in bondage in the past?

Pray: "Lord, continue to make Your truth known to me through Your Word and through Your Holy Spirit."

<><

Day Four: Through Death

Our earthly view of death tends to be so negative at times. We can't see how any type of victory can be brought forth in death — but it can. Sometimes, death is the greatest triumph of all, ending years of battling on earth to spend eternity with our heavenly Father.

PursuingGod'sWord
1 Corinthians 15:51-58

And while death can be triumphant for the individual who dies, death can also be victorious for those remaining people. Death can be the perfect portrait of what it means to serve God fully and love Him with all that we are. Death can advance His kingdom, oftentimes in ways His kingdom could never be advanced through life. Death causes us to think, resulting in a deep reflection that eventually leads us to God.

As Stephen realized he was about to be stoned, he didn't waste his breath on defending himself — he used all the breath he had to share the Gospel message of Christ. He asked the crowd and his accusers, "Which of the prophets did your fathers not persecute? And they killed those who foretold the coming of the Just One, of whom you now have become the betrayers and murderers, who have received the law by direction of angels and have not kept it" (Acts 7:51-52).

Yet in the moment of his death, Stephen was most victorious. The scene depicted in the Bible shows us a man begging for forgiveness for his unjust accusers. He said, "Lord, do not charge them with this sin" (v. 60).

Kneeling down, eyes looking upward, Stephen saw Jesus preparing to welcome him home from his time on earth. Despite their punishing stones, the people saw a man who saw Jesus. They could deny the validity of heaven and Jesus as being the Messiah all they wanted, but they could not deny the fact that Stephen saw Him.

The people were given another chance to see God's love for them through Stephen's death.

What a testimony Stephen gave for God! Instead of his last words being vindictive and angry over the apparent injustice occurring at the Lord's feet, Stephen sought to lift the Lord up — and give convicting and encouraging words to the people who could hear him.

Stephen understood the Gospel message, which enabled him to clearly and more effectively advance God's kingdom. However, it was through his death that Stephen conveyed the message of truth in action. In case they missed Jesus' death on the Cross, the people were given another chance to see God's love for them through Stephen's death.

Sometimes, it is difficult for us to imagine the good that can come from death. We cannot live in terror that God will strike us down once we begin to grow in our faith. His life, His death, and His resurrection are all tangible examples of just how much He loves us.

As we seek to advance the kingdom of God, we must not forget how He can advance His kingdom, both in life and death.

Christ's Heart in You

1. How have you seen God move through someone's death?

2. How have you been impacted by the death of someone you've known?

Pray: "Lord, give me a deeper understanding of Your Word and help me to see how Your Kingdom is advanced, even in death."

<><

Day Five: Through Rebirth

People can argue theology until they run out of breath, but they cannot argue with personal experience. When the Holy Spirit moves in our lives in dramatic fashion, the naysayers can continue to disagree with our theology, but they can't disavow what God has done.

Pursuing**God's**Word
Acts 9:10-22

When it comes to advancing God's kingdom, a powerful tool is our rebirth. Leaving the darkness behind and walking anew in the light of the truth is undeniable to those around us who have seen how we were and now how we are. God does not waste any energy — His every move in some way, however discreet or obvious, accomplishes His plans and purposes on earth. Our salvation is all part of that plan.

As adamant as Paul was against the Gospel of Jesus Christ, it was difficult for those in the new Christian community to believe that he had actually converted. To the new believers, the possibility of Paul's conversion had to seem like the wildest of dreams — one of the chief persecutors of the new Christian faith accepting Christ as the Messiah?

His every move in some way, however discreet or obvious, accomplishes His plans and purposes on earth.

The believers had to believe Paul's conversion was authentic — those who had yet to receive Jesus as the Son of God were probably captivated by his passion about this new revelation in his life. They had no reason to reject Paul's teaching. However, they could relate to the former lifestyle which Paul lived. And they could share in his stories of emptiness before Christ. Yet the religious sect of the Jews wanted Paul (then called Saul) dead.

"Then all who heard were amazed, and said, 'Is this not he who destroyed those who called on this name in Jerusalem, and has come here for that purpose, so that he might bring them bound to the chief priests?' But Saul increased all the more in strength, and confounded the Jews who dwelt in Damascus, proving that this Jesus is the Christ" (Acts 9:21-22).

From his personal rebirth experience, Paul wrote this to the church in Corinth: "Therefore, if anyone is in Christ, he is a new creation; old things have passed away; behold, all things have become new" (2 Corinthians 5:17).

Paul could attest to this truth in his own life — and the world around him couldn't deny it. At one point in his life, Paul was dragging Christians before the religious rulers and overseeing their deaths. Now, he was preaching about the death of a man named Jesus who had suddenly changed Paul's reason for living — it had given Paul a reason to live.

Our testimonies, no matter how powerful they may or may not seem, advance God's kingdom in ways we will never know. By living a life transformed by Christ, our perspective changes, allowing us to see things like God sees them. In the process, our hearts are ultimately changed forever — and the people we meet cannot deny the power that has forever transformed us.

Christ's Heart in You

1. How has your own journey into a relationship with Christ impacted those around you?

2. How can your testimony demonstrate the power of God at work in your own life?

Pray: "Lord, help me to continue to pursue You and advance Your Kingdom as You transform my heart."

<><

Your Pursuit

A Holy Heart

Few delights can equal the mere presence of One whom we fully trust.
— George MacDonald

Day One: Compassion

When we reflect on our hearts, we often-times uncover the darkness buried deep beneath the surface. While others

PursuingGod'sWord
Colossians 3:12-17

may think we have it all together, we know what lies underneath the slick veneer that we portray — and we don't like it. We want to change, as we desperately seek answers on how our heart can align with God's Word.

The Apostle Paul, a man who saw his heart transformed from one of utter darkness to radiant light, outlined what a holy heart should look like: "So, as those who have been chosen of God, holy and beloved, put on a heart of compassion, kindness, humility, gentleness and patience" (Colossians 3:12).

For most people, compassion doesn't come easily. While human nature has an enormous capacity for compassion, more often than not we're moved to casual concern rather than love in action. We pity the plight of the poor victim, yet we never do anything about it.

Can we pray for someone? Can we help someone in any form or fashion? Can we offer our homes, our lives, our resources? True compassion takes concern and elevates it to the level where you leave the stands for the playing field.

In the movie "Field of Dreams," Archie "Moonlight" Graham is a character who played one game in the major leagues. However, he never had the opportunity to bat. He left baseball to become a doctor, but returned to the field of dreams for a chance to play a full game, including getting to bat.

True compassion takes concern and elevates it to the level where you leave the stands for the playing field.

In an unfortunate turn of events, the main character, Ray, watches helpless as his daughter begins choking on a hot dog. Graham knows he can help, but is faced with the dilemma of crossing the line to help Ray's daughter and save her life or staying to finish the game. Graham barely hesitates before he crosses the line and saves her life.

Jesus scarcely hesitated either when He recognized a need. "As He stepped ashore, He saw a huge crowd, felt compassion for them, and healed their sick" (Matthew 14:14).

To have a heart that's holy, we must assume the posture that is completely selfless. Compassion is altruistic, as is Christianity. Jesus was never concerned about Himself — it was His disciples or the people around Him or the sick or the poor or the needy. He didn't even come to earth for Himself — He came for others.

To have a heart that's full of compassion, we must come before God with open hands and boldness — boldness to ask Him to undo the selfish nature of our flesh that hinders us from being filled with godly compassion.

Christ's Heart in You

1. What moves you to action when you see helpless people?

2. How can you respond more Christ-like when you see injustices in the world?

Pray: "Lord, show me what action to take when I see people in helpless situations."

<><

Day Two: Kindness

In cleansing our heart and putting on a heart that's holy, we are faced with some difficult choices. The problem is not that we wouldn't love to be kind people — the problem is our flesh tends to rise up and attempt to stamp out all our good will and intentions. How do we choose God's way over our flesh in an obvious struggle over conflicting values?

PursuingGod'sWord
James 2:1-13

A holy heart, one that is kind in nature, will begin to shelve its rights. So often, we hold on to our rights — and our right to hold onto them. While we may understand that we should react kindly toward others in certain situations, we realize that we would have to forfeit our rights.

If we are to be a people whose hearts are holy, exuding kindness at every turn, we must be willing to surrender our rights. What's so important about our ways or our claims that we must be the champion in every situation? What about championing the cause of Christ by making others first in all that we do?

We must be willing to surrender all our rights for the sake of the Gospel.

Jesus' very life exemplified kindness in each situation. People couldn't escape His kindness, not even the Pharisees. He would make no distinction in sharing God's love. He spoke under the guise of night with some Pharisees who had questions about salvation. He openly entered into fellowship with some of the dregs of Jewish society. He laid down His rights to be correct and uphold the law in every situation — He upheld grace.

The scene of Jesus with the adulteress woman is a powerful one that demonstrates how kindness overrides the status quo. A group of men chased the woman through the street, itching to stone her for her sin. But when they brought her before Jesus, He invoked kindness like she surely had never experienced. Jesus told the woman, "Neither do I condemn you; go. From now on sin no more" (John 8:11).

God's heart is for grace, for "mercy triumphs over judgment" (James 2:13).

If we desire to have hearts that are holy, hearts that are oozing with kindness instead of harsh judgment, we must be willing to surrender all our rights for the sake of the Gospel. People in the world must see that as followers of Christ we are committed to living out the traits of God that drew us to Him — compassion, kindness, gentleness, grace, and mercy. And a heart that's kind, yielding in its very manner, does just that.

The apostle Paul writes, "And be kind and compassionate to one another, forgiving one another, just as God also forgave you in Christ" (Ephesians 4:32).

Christ's Heart in You

1. How can you be more kind to those around you?

2. How have you experienced kindness recently in your life?

Pray: "Lord, fill my heart with kindness for those around me."

<><

Day Three: Gentleness

By our human nature, we want justice. We want to see the righteous side prevail and those who are trying to cheat the system appropriately punished. It's what makes us cheer at the end of a movie where an unjust fate has befallen the hero and he finally wins in the end.

PursuingGod'sWord
Galatians 6

So often in our spiritual lives, the thirst for justice nearly consumes us. We want to put on our Junior Holy Spirit badge and arrest all those hypocritical Christians out there. We'd like to see fire called down from heaven on a select few people as we wonder if God sees what they're getting away with.

While the desire to see justice prevail isn't wrong, the idea that we must be the ones handling the conviction of the body of Christ is counterproductive. God has a mechanism for accomplishing this task in the person of the Holy Spirit. The Holy Spirit convicts us and stirs our hearts to do God's will. He also challenges us to do what's right, even if it's the most difficult thing to do.

Instead of zapping people with our conviction — which all too often feels like condemnation — we should shower them with gentleness as we lovingly restore them after they've fallen. Most people know when they've done wrong and they don't need another person standing over them affirming that fact. What most people need is someone to gently usher them back to a place of health and maturity in their relationship with Christ.

To have a holy heart, we must embrace the characteristic of gentleness, recognizing that Jesus was gentle in the way He conducted Himself. So often, we misconstrue gentleness for weakness, when, in fact, just the opposite is true. It takes much strength to be gentle.

What most people need is someone to gently usher them back to a place of health and maturity in their relationship with Christ.

The apostle Paul writes, "If someone is caught in any wrongdoing, you who are spiritual should restore such a person with a gentle spirit, watching out for yourselves so you won't be tempted also" (Galatians 6:1).

To approach a broken heart with soft hands is going to be much more fruitful than grabbing someone and shaking the ever-loving life out of them until they "get it." We, too, are not beyond falling on such points, and if we keep that perspective before us, hopefully that pure heart will exude through our relationships with others.

Our desire to have a heart that's holy includes approaching others with gentleness. People don't need to be condemned — they need to be loved.

Consider what James writes about God's wisdom: "But the wisdom from above is first pure, then peace-loving, gentle, compliant, full of mercy and good fruits, without favoritism and hypocrisy" (James 3:17).

Christ's Heart in You

1. How can you be more gentle in your relationships?

2. How have you seen gentleness extended to you?

Pray: "Lord, give me a gentle spirit so I may show others a part of Your heart for mankind."

<><

Day Four: Patience

There are moments in life where our memory is shorter than a New York minute. For some reason, we can't recall the time in our life where we were just bumbling along, faltering every other step and struggling to understand what God was trying to teach us. Perhaps we are there now; perhaps we aren't.

Pursuing**God's**Word
2 Timothy 4:1-2

Regardless of how close or how far we are from God right now, we must understand the importance of patience, for it takes patience to grow ourselves and it takes patience with others to walk them to a place of maturity. However, it's often a great source of our frustration, no matter where we are coming from.

Patience develops holiness in our lives by cleansing us from our demands and desires for God to meet our timing.

The state of holiness in our hearts is weighted heavily on how willing we are to remain patient in allowing God to work in us or in those around us. One of our biggest mistakes is rushing a perfect God. Whether it's in our lives or the lives of our friends and family, we want an instant result. We want to know what direction to take now. We want to know the future now. We want someone to experience a changed life. We want desperately to see someone we know find Jesus.

Jesus, however, demonstrated a holy heart in the way that patience emanated from every part of His life.

Jesus' disciples were not the fastest bunch of men. They exasperated Jesus from time to time. On occasion, He even questioned aloud when they were ever going to get what He was saying. But did Jesus stop loving them? Did He stop reaching out to them and imparting His wisdom and knowledge to them?

Patience develops holiness in our lives by cleansing us from our demands and desires for God to meet our timing. A heart that's holy acknowledges the lordship of Jesus in each and every situation, including that of timing for our lives and the lives of those around us.

Though it may sound extreme, we act as if we know better than God when we demand that He reveal something or act in a certain way regarding our lives. Holiness says, "God, You know best — do it Your way in Your time. Your will be done."

The apostle Paul noticed a large number of leaders in the early church were not trusting that God would mature the flock. They thought they had to do it themselves. But in their immature attitudes toward others, Paul made it clear what they should do: "Proclaim the message; persist in it whether convenient or not; rebuke, correct, and encourage with great patience and teaching" (2 Timothy 4:2).

The way we encourage others is through patience and sharing the wisdom God has given to us. And if we honor God in this way, allowing Him to work in His timing both in our lives and the lives of others, He will do amazing things through us, with us, and in us.

Christ's Heart in You

1. How does your impatience affect your relationship with God? with others?

2. How can you be more patient with God and other people?

Pray: "Lord, give me a heart that patiently waits on You to do Your will."

Day Five: True Holiness

Jesus' piercing glare could see deep into the windows of men's souls when He walked the earth. And the Lord still looks upon us in that same manner today. Beyond our exteriors — pure or dirty in appearance — rests our hearts, the tale-telling state of our souls. And it's there that God sees whether or not the holiness we attempt to perpetrate is genuine or contrived.

> **PursuingGod'sWord**
> Leviticus 11:44

The Pharisees were always seeking to refute Jesus as He went around performing miracle after miracle. What they saw was an unschooled scholar who didn't appear to live a life of holiness according to their standards. They looked upon Jesus in the natural.

Of course, at first glance, they may have been just in their accusations — that is, just if your measuring stick is one of strict rules and regulations with no margin of error. The Law was their guidebook and never could they deviate from it.

What the Pharisees missed was that Jesus never erred, staying within the intent of the law as He displayed a loving touch to everyone He met. Jesus desired to save, to heal, to restore, to help, to love. Jesus didn't shirk the Law, but He knew that following every letter of it alone could not bring about the level of holiness the Pharisees believed they had obtained.

Holiness isn't merely refraining from sin. Holiness is a reaction to the living God.

On the Sabbath, Jesus went into the synagogue and was teaching when He spotted a man with a withered hand. Jesus, in His compassion and mercy, wanted to heal the man's hand. Much to the ire of the Pharisees, Jesus commanded the man to stretch out his hand — and it was healed.

The Pharisees believed this was work. Jesus wanted to know why they believed it was wrong for Him to do good on the Lord's day. Could He not do good and refrain from work at the same time?

Gary L. Thomas writes: "The holiness God wants is a holiness rooted in Christ's death and resurrection, a holiness that changes our hearts, not just our actions."

The outer holiness that the Pharisees portrayed was commanding. They were stalwarts of holiness, demonstrating to those around them what it meant to live a pure life. But their religion was dead. The God whom they claimed to worship was not alive in their hearts and thoughts. The holiness they possessed was a facade.

In Leviticus 11:44, God tells the people of Israel to "be holy, for I am holy," and Peter reiterates that cry for holiness in the New Testament.

Holiness isn't merely refraining from sin.

Holiness is a reaction to the living God. It's when we come to a place where we realize that we want to be holy just as He is holy. We should not desire to be holy for holiness' sake. We want to be changed men and women of God whose hearts are bent on serving Him and bring nothing but glory to His awesome name, something a heart entrenched in the holiness of a cold law could never fully glorify.

Christ's Heart in You

1. Does your relationship with God continue to change your heart or just your actions? Why?

2. What are some traits of the Pharisees you see in your own life? Pray and ask God to remove those from your heart.

Pray: "Lord, I want to have a holy heart, full of Your love, mercy, peace, and compassion. Let my heart be changed as You transform me through Your holiness."

<><

Your Pursuit

The Author

Jason Chatraw is the small groups pastor at the Atlanta Vineyard Church and has a passion for helping people deepen their relationship with God. He has served as the assistant editor for Dr. Charles Stanley's *In Touch* magazine before moving into full-time ministry.

Jason graduated from the University of Georgia with a Bachelor of Arts degree in Newspaper Journalism. He worked as a sports writer and sports editor at newspapers in South Carolina and Georgia before entering into the ministry.

He has written articles for a number of Christian publications and is a regular contributor to *Stand Firm* magazine.

Jason lives in Atlanta with his wife Janel. To contact Jason, you can write him at 6920 Jimmy Carter Blvd., Suite 200, Norcross, GA 30071 or you can e-mail him at jason.chatraw@atlantavineyard.com.